YOUR YEAR
(YOUR VERSION)

INSPIRED BY

Taylor Swift

A GUIDED JOURNAL AND PLANNER

YOUR YEAR
(YOUR VERSION)

UNOFFICIAL AND UNAUTHORIZED

SARAH O'HARA

PLUME

PLUME

An imprint of Penguin Random House LLC
1745 Broadway, New York, NY 10019
penguinrandomhouse.com

First published in Great Britain in 2024 by Seven Dials, an imprint of
The Orion Publishing Group Ltd. This edition published in the United States of
America in 2025 by Plume, an imprint of Penguin Random House LLC.
Copyright © 2024 by The Orion Publishing Group

Illustrations on pages 71, 74, 75, 81, 85, 87 and 88
© Rachael Lancaster / The Orion Publishing Group.
All other illustrations © Shutterstock

LIBRARY OF CONGRESS CONTROL NUMBER: 2025938297

ISBN 9798217177622 (paperback)

Printed in the United States of America
1st Printing

The authorized representative in the EU for product safety and compliance is
Penguin Random House Ireland, Morrison Chambers, 32 Nassau Street,
Dublin D02 YH68, Ireland, https://eu-contact.penguin.ie.

Contents

Welcome

to *Your Year (Your Version)*, the Taylor Swift–inspired guided journal and planner.

With twelve months, twelve eras, and twelve albums, *Your Year (Your Version)* is created to inspire you to live the life you want—your year, your way, your version.

The following pages will guide you through structuring your plans, thoughts, and reflections as you navigate the coming months and enter each of your own different eras, helping you to curate the best year you can.

Inspired by the words and wisdom of Taylor Swift, travel from January (*reputation*) to December (*Midnights*) with seasonal prompts for goal-setting, honing your personal aims, and building new habits.

Let the music of Taylor inspire you as you enter your year, your version.

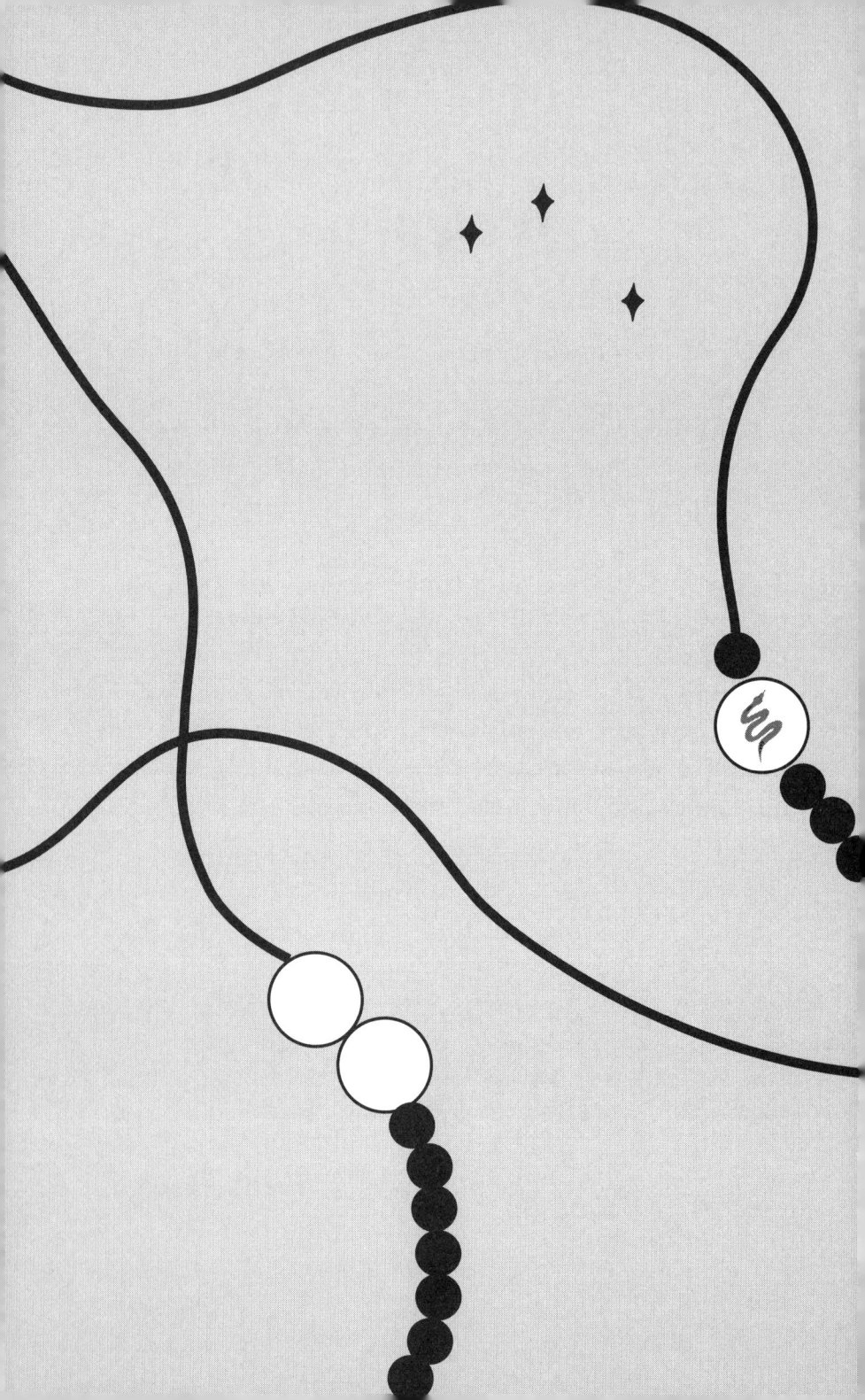

January

Introduction

January is *reputation*.

The deepest, bitterest slice of winter. With the lights and sounds of the festive season dimming, it often feels like there's nothing to distract us from the dark nights and the biting cold. But we can find new beginnings within January, alongside the clarity that comes from endings.

When *reputation* was released in 2017, it signaled to some that Taylor was facing the end of something herself: the narrative that painted her as the world's favorite wholesome pop singer. With a startling new energy, sound, and aesthetic, Taylor leaned into the messiness of her new-found vulnerability with *reputation*.

She embraced the new, letting go of the old.

With New Year's resolutions and the "New Year, New Me" mantra that many embrace come January, the month can feel full of promise; loud and bombastic, a deliberate disavowal of who we once were for who we want to become.

January is also about hunkering down with the things and people that mean the most to us, as Taylor does on some of *reputation*'s quieter moments. We can declare big intentions, embrace a new us, be fully certain of the ways we've changed—alongside these calmer thoughts and experiences with those we love. Taylor so often presents the duality of living, the two (sometimes conflicting) sides of what it means to really lead a complex and messy life. We are never just one thing. The image of Taylor on the cover of the *reputation* album is stripped back and pared-down—black and white, her hair wet and tousled, the newspaper font glitching behind her, disregarded and fading into the background.

Leading up to *reputation*, Taylor deleted all of her social media channels and was barely seen in public for a year. This was such a huge switch from the activity—both online and offline—that had characterized her *1989* era. We all need, sometimes, to reset.

January can be the perfect time to tune out the noise and find your own peace. Clarify what you want to achieve this year—for you and you alone—and what no longer matters too. Like *reputation*, a reset can be exhilarating in its harshness.

January is for shedding your past like a snakeskin.

As Taylor reflects in the album's prologue: "We think we know someone, but the truth is that we only know the version of them they have chosen to show us." It can feel revolutionary to acknowledge the power of this and to understand that, sometimes, other people will misinterpret us. And yet, as Taylor notes in some of *reputation*'s more self-doubting moments, the past is harder to escape than we might like to admit and we can't always control how we're perceived. It can feel like "dancing with our hands tied" when we choose to start again, in the context of whatever our past year might have felt like.

There are two sides to *reputation,* the light and the dark—the intrusive and untrue media narrative of a life versus Taylor's personal experience. The album manages to simultaneously represent and reflect on the quietest and the loudest periods of her life, and so this month is about finding a balance within the tension. Where you have been matters to where you are—that's unavoidable. But finding peace with the past is the only way to carve a new path—however narrow and winding, however messy and vulnerable—to the new year.

January is a key time to assess your life in different ways. Over the month, reflect on the last year—both its failures and successes—and set goals for what you want to achieve this year. Use the habit tracker to identify and map out three habits that can help you start off toward these goals in a sustainable way.

You can address whichever areas of your life that you want. Or, as Taylor does in *reputation*, completely change your aesthetic, lifestyle, social media presence, and values. The key to achieving changes you're happy with, and setting yourself up for success, is to let go of outside perceptions of yourself.

Don't feel the need to prove yourself to anyone, or to have achieved a drastic change by the end of the month.

Revel in the small moments of peace and aim for vulnerability.

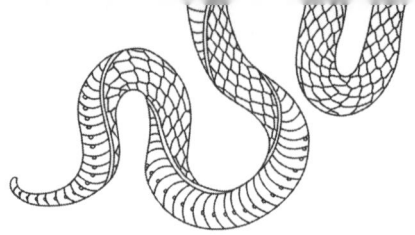

"Are you

ready
for it?"

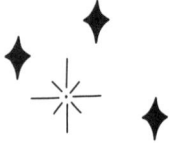 # *Goals*

This January, what do you want to leave behind and what do you want to hold on to?

Sometimes change can feel both inevitable and forced upon you, but it might just be exactly what you need. What changes have you had to deal with in the past year? How can you put what you've learned into action for this year?

Think about what makes you feel powerless. Are there any actions you can take to reframe this narrative, so that you can accept your vulnerability and let go of control?

Expand under the goals below on how you will achieve each of them this month.

GOAL 1: NOURISH WHAT YOU HAVE

....

....

....

....

....

....

....

....

GOAL 2: LEARN AND DEVELOP

....

....

....

....

....

....

....

....

....

....

GOAL 3: RECLAIM YOUR POWER

....

....

....

....

....

....

....

....

reputation

reputation is an album of surprises and opposites. It starts with a huge change of sound for Taylor—announced to us immediately with the synthesizers and bass drops of "... Ready for It?" and defiant lyrics. She sings about revenge and her lack of regrets, revealing a sense that she has been pushed to this often dark, sometimes even angry, place. Yet even the album's harshest moments are accompanied by a feeling of vulnerability, as Taylor sings frequently about the unexpected, private joy she's discovered amid all the pettiness and drama that had preceded the album.

With snakes twisting over the music videos and frequent lyrical references to witches and burning, liars and actresses, the obvious aesthetics and themes of *reputation* are clear. But *reputation*'s lead singles and most well-known songs – the defiant "I Did Something Bad," the vengeful "Look What You Made Me Do," the jubilant reclaiming of her public persona in "Getaway Car"—differ hugely from the album's quieter moments.

In songs like "Delicate," "King of My Heart," and "Call It What You Want," Taylor returns to her heartfelt, softer lyrics of earlier albums as she sings about the vulnerability of fledgling relationships. Ultimately, we can't have one side of *reputation* without the other. When she sings, "my reputation's never been worse" in "Delicate," Taylor acknowledges that, even in the hardest period of her professional life, she was able to find something that she could really trust and rely on. She found it precisely because of the way her reputation and public image had suffered.

reputation ends with possibly the softest, most reflective song on the album, both lyrically and sonically: "New Year's Day." We get the sense of a turbulent period ending and an arrival at a hard-won peace. It picks up on a day which, as Taylor describes it, is not necessarily about a brand-new, fresh start.

New Year's Day can be as much about sifting through the remnants of the year before—like the glitter on the hardwood floor—as finding peace within those memories. That's *reputation*: endings and beginnings; overwhelming noise and sudden quiet; a duality of existing whereby you can pick up the broken pieces of yourself and also find something new within them.

NEW YEAR'S DAY

The first day of January is the perfect time to assess where you are right now and where you want to be in the future. Rather than forging ahead with the new, use this time to take stock of the past and look back first: "Hold on to the memories, they will hold on to you."

Look Back to Look Forward

Start the first day of this new year by reviewing your last year. Find photographs of the high and the low points; check back on any resolutions made or goals set last year. How do you feel about the year, now that the dust has settled?

Celebrate Small Wins

Find five memories of the past year you have forgotten to celebrate, and that are special only to you. These will be small, concrete moments of happiness, and they are supremely powerful because they are repeatable, easily achievable, and can act as building blocks to overall happiness. If you have photographs of them, make a collage. If not, discuss them with your friends.

Reset and Refresh

As Taylor sings in "New Year's Day," take some time to reset and refresh—whether that's tidying away and reorganizing your space, or finishing off an errand or task that's been hanging over you from last year. If you can do this with someone you love, even better—our relationships flourish through small, practical activities together as much as big, exciting, splashy events.

Lastly, before turning to what you want to change this year—which can seem so intimidating and unachievable—think about what's already going well and what you want to hold on to.

List what matters most in your life right now, and how you might nourish those same things this year.

....
....
....
....
....
....
....
....

"All the pieces fall, right into place"

HABIT TRACKER

It takes thirty days to get a habit to stick. Use January as a time to hold yourself accountable for three key habits you want to maintain. Start with the three goals you've just set on pages 10–11—can you identify an easy, buildable habit (such as journaling or setting aside time to develop a hobby) that can help you get there?

Habit 1

| 1 | 2 | 3 | 4 | 5 | 6 | 7 |
| ○ | ○ | ○ | ○ | ○ | ○ | ○ |

How's it going each week?

| 8 | 9 | 10 | 11 | 12 | 13 | 14 |
| ○ | ○ | ○ | ○ | ○ | ○ | ○ |

....

| 15 | 16 | 17 | 18 | 19 | 20 | 21 |
| ○ | ○ | ○ | ○ | ○ | ○ | ○ |

....

| 22 | 23 | 24 | 25 | 26 | 27 | 28 |
| ○ | ○ | ○ | ○ | ○ | ○ | ○ |

....

| 29 | 30 |
| ○ | ○ |

Tick each day when you have completed your habit

....

Habit 2

1	2	3	4	5	6	7
○	○	○	○	○	○	○

How's it going each week?

....

8	9	10	11	12	13	14
○	○	○	○	○	○	○

....

15	16	17	18	19	20	21
○	○	○	○	○	○	○

....

22	23	24	25	26	27	28
○	○	○	○	○	○	○

....

29	30
○	○

Tick each day when you have completed your habit

....

Habit 3

1	2	3	4	5	6	7
○	○	○	○	○	○	○

How's it going each week?

....

8	9	10	11	12	13	14
○	○	○	○	○	○	○

....

15	16	17	18	19	20	21
○	○	○	○	○	○	○

....

22	23	24	25	26	27	28
○	○	○	○	○	○	○

....

29	30
○	○

Tick each day when you have completed your habit

....

january 1-7 WEEK 1

DAY

DAY

DAY

DAY

DAY

NOTES

DAY

DAY

PRIORITIES

january 8–14 WEEK 2

DAY

DAY

DAY

DAY

DAY

NOTES

DAY

DAY

PRIORITIES

january 15–21 WEEK 3

DAY

DAY

DAY

DAY

DAY

NOTES

DAY

DAY

PRIORITIES

january 22–28 WEEK 4

DAY

DAY

DAY

DAY

DAY

NOTES

DAY

DAY

PRIORITIES

january 29–31 WEEK 5

DAY	

DAY	

DAY	

NOTES

PRIORITIES

REFLECTIONS

"Bridges burn, I never learn, at least I did one thing right"

Take a moment to look back on the first month of the year without dividing how it went into "successes" and "failures." Sometimes, to get what we want, we have to mess up. As Taylor reflects in "Call It What You Want," we can take control over our mistakes and not let them control us. Think about what hasn't gone to plan this month, and one way in which this could still help you get where you want to be. What have you learned from something that didn't go right?

"Is this the end of all the endings?"

Now that January is over, is there anything you feel you can let go of? It might be negative experiences, certain mindsets, or even things you once wanted but which no longer serve you. To achieve what we want, we must be OK with endings.

Endings are the only way to new beginnings.

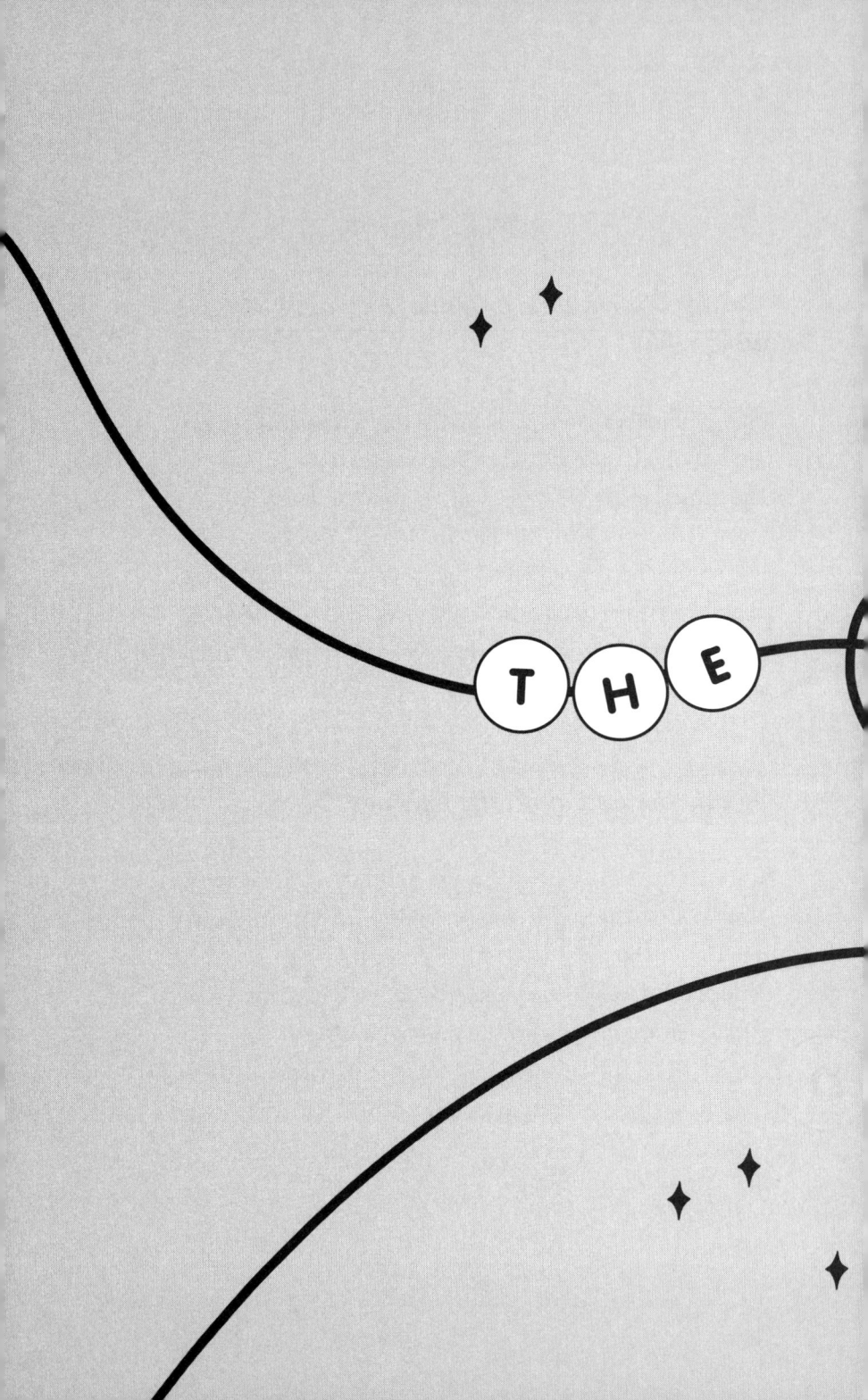

February

TORTURED POETS DEPARTMENT

Introduction

February is *The Tortured Poets Department*.
The end of winter is fast approaching and yet we can't always manage to create much hope or optimism this month. Even if you are starting to get "color back into [your] face," as Taylor sings in "So Long, London," it may not be doing much to improve your mood.

And in the middle of the dreary cold, we have Valentine's Day.

A sudden explosion of love and color—but perhaps as fleeting and transient as the moments of romantic optimism on the album, which are always dampened down by the chilly grip of self-awareness.

February can be a mixed-up month, as much as *The Tortured Poets Department* is a mixed-up album.

It's about revisiting the past and whiling away time in daydreams of a place, of a person, of a moment now long ago (maybe little more than a "Fortnight") that spawned aspirations of a different future.

But don't let this shortest of months get away from you—instead, take time to invest tangibly in your life right now.

Spring is coming, though it may not feel like it yet. We can get ready for the rest of the year, even if that's just planning an escape for the summer, as Taylor sings in "Florida!!!"

The Tortured Poets Department is a heavy album: monochrome and melancholy, filled with a lot of love and a lot of grief, restless and impatient for pain to end and growth to begin. Yet within it there are shoots of hope. Toward the end of the album, we get "The Alchemy" and with it the sense of a long-awaited, fateful return. A return to *you*.

Use the quiet, in-between spaces of this month to plant shoots for where you want to be this year.

This February is all about finding motivation and inspiration in whatever ways help you.

Whether that's jolting yourself out of bed on a Monday morning, planning a Valentine's Day activity that reflects love in whatever form it shows up for you, or just taking solace in the words of others—remember that winter is nearly over and spring is on its way.

Enjoy the warmth of the sun on your face when you start to feel it, however faint it may be. And, as Taylor does in *The Tortured Poets Department*, don't be afraid of leaning into darker, colder moments too. In those, we might find the calm we've been chasing to think in depth about who we are and where we want to be. End the month with affirmations and visualizations to help you prepare.

"All my mornings are Mondays

. . . stuck in an endless February"

MONDAY MORNINGS

When it seems like winter is never-ending, getting up and getting going can be incredibly difficult. This February, try waking up half an hour earlier each Monday morning to do one of these four activities, and start out your week in a new way.

1. **Check in with a friend.** Whether that's over a text, scheduling a ten-minute phone call, or meeting for an early-morning walk or coffee, dedicate intentional time for someone who makes you feel good.

2. **Think about and start to organize a plan for later in the week or for the weekend.** Kick off your week by giving yourself something to look forward to—and make it even better by committing to doing something new you've been meaning to for a while.

3. **Try a new hobby.** Whether it's crafty, active, or truly niche, challenge yourself to do something you've never done before.

4. **Do the thing you don't want to do the most this week.** Rather than putting off what we dread, just get it out of the way—you'll feel better for it. As Taylor says, sometimes "You gotta fake it till you make it," and she did.

The Tortured Poets Department

From the title, the track list, and the wistful, melancholy black-and-white pictures of Taylor that feature on each variant, it seemed clear to fans that her eleventh album would be a return to the break-up album.

Given the two extremely public relationships that had ended for her in 2023, the expectation was for something angry, something iconic, something powerful. And the album was all these things—but perhaps not in the way fans expected. In an era where her global profile was continually increasing, the age of Taylor's secret sessions and personal interactions with fans seemed, understandably, to be receding into the distance. But *The Tortured Poets Department* turned out to be perhaps her most intimate and vulnerable album ever, offering access into her darkest and most turbulent emotional states.

Compared to earlier albums on heartbreak—most notably 2013's *Red*—this album ends with very little sense of closure or the idea of moving on. Instead, we are invited to sit with Taylor in a mess of conflicting, beautifully realized, devastating emotions—and offered no way out of them.

The whole album feels as if the songs themselves are trapped, with upbeat music often underlying bleak lyrics; glittering, shimmering synths that refuse to calm down or abate, ensnaring Taylor in a racing heartbeat that she can't seem to settle. She is haunted by sadness in "So Long, London," where mournful lyrics sit uneasily over the pounding rhythm, and she is covered in the hollow veneer of happiness coupled with a dancy beat over clear heartbreak in "I Can Do It with a Broken Heart" and "Down Bad."

Her most starkly heartbroken song, the restrained piano ballad "loml," is marked by an agonizing uncertainty, reflected apparently even in the song title, which generated much speculation among fans when the track list was announced. Did Taylor mean "love of my life" or "loss of my life"? Both, it turns out. This is characteristic of the question that haunts the album—"what if?"—and Taylor's pulsing regret and confusion, which only breaks into clarity through startling moments of anger.

The anguished howls of songs like "Who's Afraid of Little Old Me?" or "The Smallest Man Who Ever Lived" see Taylor scream out her frustration at both personal and private wounds: the industry that has distorted her self-image ("I am what I am 'cause you trained me"), the failed relationships, and the second chances that she relives over and over.

In the album's epilogue, she describes it as 'a debrief, a detailed rewinding." From the ticking clock that symbolized much of her previous album, *Midnights*—counting down the nights to what felt, hopefully, like a kind of resolution—we now get a frantic and obsessive rewinding. It creates a sense—as exemplified by the double album release of *The Anthology* the same night—that this is something Taylor just can't let go of.

It's also an album that focuses deeply on Taylor's relationship with her fans, coming out as it did when speculation about her personal life was at a height not reached since the days of *1989*. In her angrier moments, she lashes out at those who have "clutched their pearls" at her, but the album's closer, "Clara Bow," takes a more wry, analytical approach. With a structure that builds over three verses, taking us through comparisons to three "It girls" of different eras (Clara Bow, Stevie Nicks, and finally Taylor herself), it ends on an unnamed subject compared flatteringly to Taylor, but with more "edge."

Invoking a criticism that the former Nashville sweetheart has faced her whole career, we get a sense of an artist and a woman who has matured past the quaking fear at the heart of *Red*'s "Nothing New": someone calmly aware that in the world of fame, you're always replaceable.

Tortured Poetry

"You're not Dylan Thomas, I'm not Patti Smith"
There are references to famous writers throughout Taylor's lyrics, from Emily Dickinson, to Wordsworth, to Patti Smith. Pick one of the poems below to read—ideally while cozily inside on a cold, dark February night—and think about how the way Taylor uses it might be completely different from the writer's initial intentions.

Can you apply the poem's themes, emotions, and words to your own life?

Do not go gentle into that good night—Dylan Thomas
A Wife—at daybreak I shall be (461)—Emily Dickinson
I Wandered Lonely as a Cloud—William Wordsworth

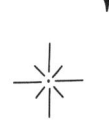

HOW DOES LOVE SHOW UP IN YOUR LIFE?

Plan something to mark Valentine's Day that reflects love to you—not how it might appear to anyone else.

Who makes you feel the most loved? How do they show up for you?

There are many different kinds of love in *The Tortured Poets Department*, some heavy and painful. But there's also the love of a place, a break, an escape, that we get in "Florida!!!" There's the "once every few lifetimes" love that Taylor sings about in "The Alchemy." And beneath the grief of the album, there's a palpable love and protection of Taylor herself, sharing with us an acceptance that you can only let yourself be sad for so long.

How can you make yourself feel loved this Valentine's Day? Plan a celebration with friends, family, or loved ones to celebrate your favorite things about them.

♡ *Affirmations*

For one week in February, try repeating these affirmations to yourself. This can be done however feels most natural—journaling at night before you sleep, or saying them out loud to your reflection in the mirror first thing in the morning.

I am loved.

Love shows up freely in my life.

I love with my whole heart.

I deserve love.

Visualizations

Is there somewhere you routinely go to in your daydreams? Do you have a goal you imagine yourself achieving, a place you'd like to live, or even a past event that you imagine happening differently?

Take yourself into this recurring daydream and write it down. Add as many details as you have in your head, with no feeling and certainly no embarrassment.

Read it back. Can you spot why this particular daydream appeals to you? Are there ways to tangibly achieve it, or to replicate the feeling it gives you?

Don't get stuck in daydreams and fantasies. Use concrete visualizations of where you want to be later in the year to plant the "shoots" in February that will soon flower.

Imagine yourself six months from now. What does your life look like? What's different in your routines and the average day? What steps would it take for you to get there?

"Staring at the sky, come back and pick me up"

SOMETHING DIFFERENT I'D DO EACH DAY IS . . .

....

....

....

....

....

....

....

....

SOMETHING I WOULD LIKE TO WORK TOWARD IS . . .

....

....

....

....

....

....

....

....

....

....

february 1-7 WEEK 1

DAY

DAY

DAY

DAY

DAY	NOTES

DAY	

DAY	PRIORITIES

february 8-14 WEEK 2

DAY

DAY

DAY

DAY

DAY

NOTES

DAY

DAY

PRIORITIES

february 15–21 WEEK 3

DAY

DAY

DAY

DAY

DAY

NOTES

DAY

DAY

PRIORITIES

february 22-28 WEEK 4

DAY

DAY

DAY

DAY

DAY

NOTES

DAY

DAY

PRIORITIES

DAY

february 29 WEEK 5

DAY

NOTES

PRIORITIES

OVERVIEW

Here are some questions to reflect on at the end of this month:

★ *How did February go for you?*

★ *Celebrate one thing you're proud of.*

★ *Acknowledge and let go of anything that went less well.*

★ *Set aside an afternoon to finish off any quick tasks or errands from this month, reset your space, and set your intentions and goals for the month ahead.*

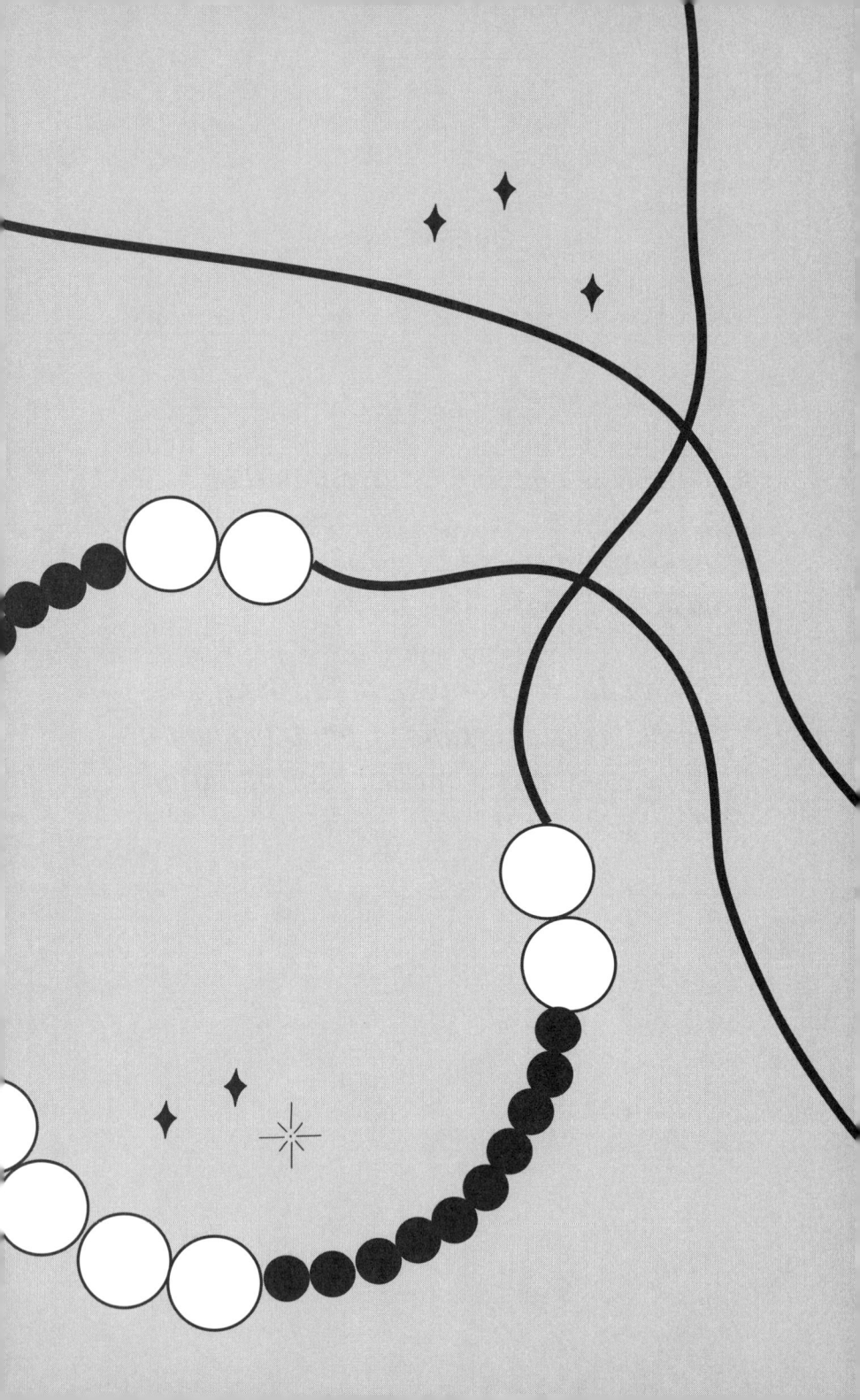

March

Introduction

March is *Speak Now*.

Spring is here.

With it—sudden showers, bursts of sun. Change, growth, loss, the heartbreaking speed with which flowers and birdsong can stream into the world again. As Taylor describes in the prologue to *Speak Now (Taylor's Version)*, this is an album for both the "most emotionally turbulent" and the "most idealistic, hopeful" times in your life. This is an album for spring.

With the onrush of hope, joy, and newfound innocence can come startling reminders of loss—of how quickly life can change. *Speak Now* embraces turbulence and uncertainty, and all it asks of you is that you feel these feelings completely. It has a fairy-tale design with castles, dragons, and princesses, brave hopes and big dreams, and tragic, dramatic betrayals. It's the last gasps of innocence and romance, and, with its tears, sunshine, and dramatic storms, it is spring.

Spring can be a time to take stock of and reclaim your strength, your own voice. That's what Taylor did, aged nineteen, facing reviews and media that diminished her abilities as a songwriter and a storyteller, constantly giving credit to her cowriters. She heard those words, sat down, and wrote an album entirely by herself, with no one else who could possibly be credited with her accomplishments.

In doing that, she knew she would be exposing one of her biggest vulnerabilities: what if she couldn't write alone? What if, as detractors claimed, her cowriters had been the reason for previous successes? Wouldn't she be setting herself up to fail?

These are the kinds of questions that, if we let them, will paralyze us and deter us from changing. But it's March now, and the world is waking up. Shake up your life with it.

Speak Now is about just that: claiming who you are and what you think as publicly and as loudly as you want to. In all its messiness and constant revisions, spring is a time for trying things out, seeing if they suit you, and throwing them out again if they don't make you feel *you*.

This spring, wear those bright colors. Get rid of things you no longer use along with thought patterns that no longer help you. Never be ashamed of your feelings—instead, be thankful for the full spectrum of emotions, from hope to rage to regret, that you get to feel.

Stand in the pouring rain. Embrace the uncertainty of the weather, the seasons, the sun, and the showers. Let yourself revel in all the possibilities, as frightening as they might be and, in fact, pick the possibility that frightens you most. Find a voice for yourself and speak now.

Use March to embrace uncertainty and the new, and take some time for physical, mental, and emotional spring cleaning.

You can decide what takes up space in your life. To prepare yourself for change and new chapters, you may need to make room for new things, whether that's in your physical space or in your life.

Over the month, clear out the habits or thoughts you no longer need, and leave yourself room for lots of feelings. Embrace the changing of the seasons and identify what might be holding you back.

"This was the

very
first
page"

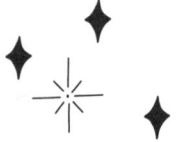 # *Goals*

With a new season comes the opportunity for fresh starts and renewal. Spring comes each year and yet it can still feel like a shock to the system. With all you've learned this winter, look back on the goals you set in January (see pages 10–11).

How do you feel about them now? Do any of them need adjusting based on the way you're living your life?

GOAL 1: NOURISH WHAT YOU HAVE

....

....

....

....

....

....

....

....

....

....

GOAL 2: LEARN AND DEVELOP

....

....

....

....

....

....

....

....

....

....

GOAL 3: RECLAIM YOUR POWER

....

....

....

....

....

....

....

....

Speak Now

At first glance, *Speak Now*'s title track feels slightly disconnected from what is, overall, a very direct and confessional album. Taylor describes it in the liner notes as a concept album of "open letters," with each song "written with a specific person in mind, telling them what I meant to tell them in person."

"Speak Now" stands out as a more obviously metaphorical song, employing some of the heady run-away-with-me romanticism of Taylor's previous album, *Fearless*, as the song fantasizes about stopping a wedding at the last possible moment.

Really, though, "Speak Now" encapsulates all that this album is about: bravery, forthrightness, and the feeling that perhaps it's better to live with the mistakes we have made than regret for the things we never did.

Speak Now sits in between the country sound and girl-next-door sensibilities of Taylor's first two albums, and the experimentation with different genres and more mature lyrics that would come with *Red* and *1989*. It is crafted with some of the fairy-tale whimsy of *Fearless* —floating ballgowns, lyrics about fighting dragons, and sparkling evenings—but with a more mature, realistic sensibility. The Taylor of *Speak Now* knows that things might go wrong, even as she sings about her hopes that they'll go right.

The album holds many contrasting emotions at once: gracious forgiveness in "Innocent," a sense of often-revisited regret in "Back to December," strident anger in "Better than Revenge," and stunned, devastated heartbreak in "Last Kiss." In "Sparks Fly," she longs for all-consuming love—for fireworks and something to haunt her—but in "Haunted" and "Dear John," we see the bitter tail-end of this passion.

In this space between adolescence and adulthood, the fairy-tale visions of love and life are almost, but not quite entirely, smashed into a million contradictory shards of emotions. It's the frailty of what keeps them together that makes *Speak Now* such a nostalgic album for so many fans.

The original track listing finishes with "Long Live," where we return to the high school metaphors of her previous hit single "You Belong with Me." The fairy-tale imagery sprinkled through *Speak Now* is at its clearest here, but beneath the lyrics we find a more grounded, assured Taylor. She seems to lean for the first time on her artistry and the community she has built for herself, recognizing her own achievements. It's an album where she moves ever closer to extreme vulnerability, and a reminder that only through seasons of change can we find stability.

"I had the time of my life fighting dragons with you"

Spring Clean

Spring is the season of renewal, of shedding winter layers and increasing energy and activity. Cleaning and clearing can help us feel more in control and intentional with our life.

Use this seasonal shift to declutter and spring clean physically, emotionally, and mentally.

"Drop everything now"

PHYSICAL SPRING CLEAN

Spring Cleaning Activity: Wardrobe

Go through your wardrobe and pick out the clothes that make you feel the most comfortable and confident. After your January reset, are there any that you feel no longer reflect your personality or style? Donate or repurpose them to clear out your space and freshen up your wardrobe.

Spring Cleaning Activity: Routines

When decluttering your space, think about rearranging it to make it easier for you to stick to the habits and routines that help you.

For instance, is there enough space to help you get ready in the mornings, like a place to set out what you need the night before? Could you make a comfy corner for reading and journaling, if that's something you want to do more of? If you're trying to get

into the habit of morning and night routines, see if you can make a small station, laying out what you want to do, like sticky notes for affirmations or headphones for meditation.

"So I'll watch your life in pictures"

MENTAL SPRING CLEAN

With so much life now lived online, a physical spring clean may not help lift a feeling of mental clutter. Take the time to go through the online spaces and devices that take up the most of your time, and refresh and reset them.

Are there pages or profiles you return to out of envy or sadness? If so, could you mute or unfollow them?

Are there pictures you could archive or delete on your phone? Alternatively, if you can never find pictures or mementos because your camera roll feels too disorganized, try clearing out duplicated pictures and screenshots, so you can more easily find the important stuff.

Try setting screen-time limits or intentions for use of social media.

"I go back to December all the time"

EMOTIONAL SPRING CLEAN

If there are memories or emotional states you find yourself stuck in, take time to journal about them. Reflect on what you could have done differently in those times. Can you identify why you continually return to this thought process and the ways it might be holding you back? How can you give yourself the grace to let this go?

Season of Innocence and Loss

"Don't you think I was too young to be messed with?"

The new growth and change that spring brings can serve as a reminder of loss, as well as innocence. Sometimes, with age and growth, we can feel huge sadness for our younger selves, and perhaps miss the carefree attitude we once had.

Taylor seems to revisit the emotions of "Dear John" in her later album *Midnights*, with lyrical parallels between the earlier song and "Would've, Could've, Should've." In the interaction between these two songs, we see a new perspective gained, and while Taylor's self-blame has been put aside, in some ways it seems like her anger at the situation has only increased.

Take some time outside, observing the new life now present in nature, and check in with how you feel. What effect do new flowers, leaves, and birdsong have on you? How do the changing seasons help you reflect on your own growth?

"It's okay, life is a tough crowd"

When *Speak Now* was first released, the song "Innocent" seemed to
reference a now-infamous moment at the MTV Video Music Awards.
In the song, Taylor extends forgiveness and understanding, seeking
to close a chapter that would end up being reopened again and again
throughout her career. With a much-reported media feud now lying
between the original song and her re-recording, her maturer voice—
deeper, smoother, more controlled—seems more self-reflective. At
the time of the re-recording, Taylor is in her thirties, the age she was
singing about "*still growin' up*" in, and she is still feeling the after-
effects of this interaction on her career all these years later.

Sometimes, we need to forgive others; other times, we have to do
the harder work of forgiving ourselves. Either way, don't let anger or
shame burden you.

Have you ever felt that you've extended forgiveness and not felt the
benefits of it? Rather than regretting this, try extending that same
forgiveness and compassion to yourself.

march 1–7 WEEK 1

DAY

DAY

DAY

DAY

DAY

NOTES

DAY

DAY

PRIORITIES

march 8-14 WEEK 2

DAY

DAY

DAY

DAY

DAY

NOTES

DAY

DAY

PRIORITIES

march 15–21 WEEK 3

DAY

DAY

DAY

DAY

DAY

NOTES

DAY

DAY

PRIORITIES

march 22–28 WEEK 4

DAY

DAY

DAY

DAY

DAY

NOTES

DAY

DAY

PRIORITIES

march 29-31 WEEK 5

DAY	

NOTES

DAY	

DAY	

PRIORITIES

OVERVIEW

Here are some questions to reflect on at the end of this month:

★ *How did March go for you?*

★ *Celebrate one thing you're proud of.*

★ *Acknowledge and let go of anything that went less well.*

★ *Set aside an afternoon to finish off any quick tasks or errands from this month, reset your space, and set your intentions and goals for the month ahead.*

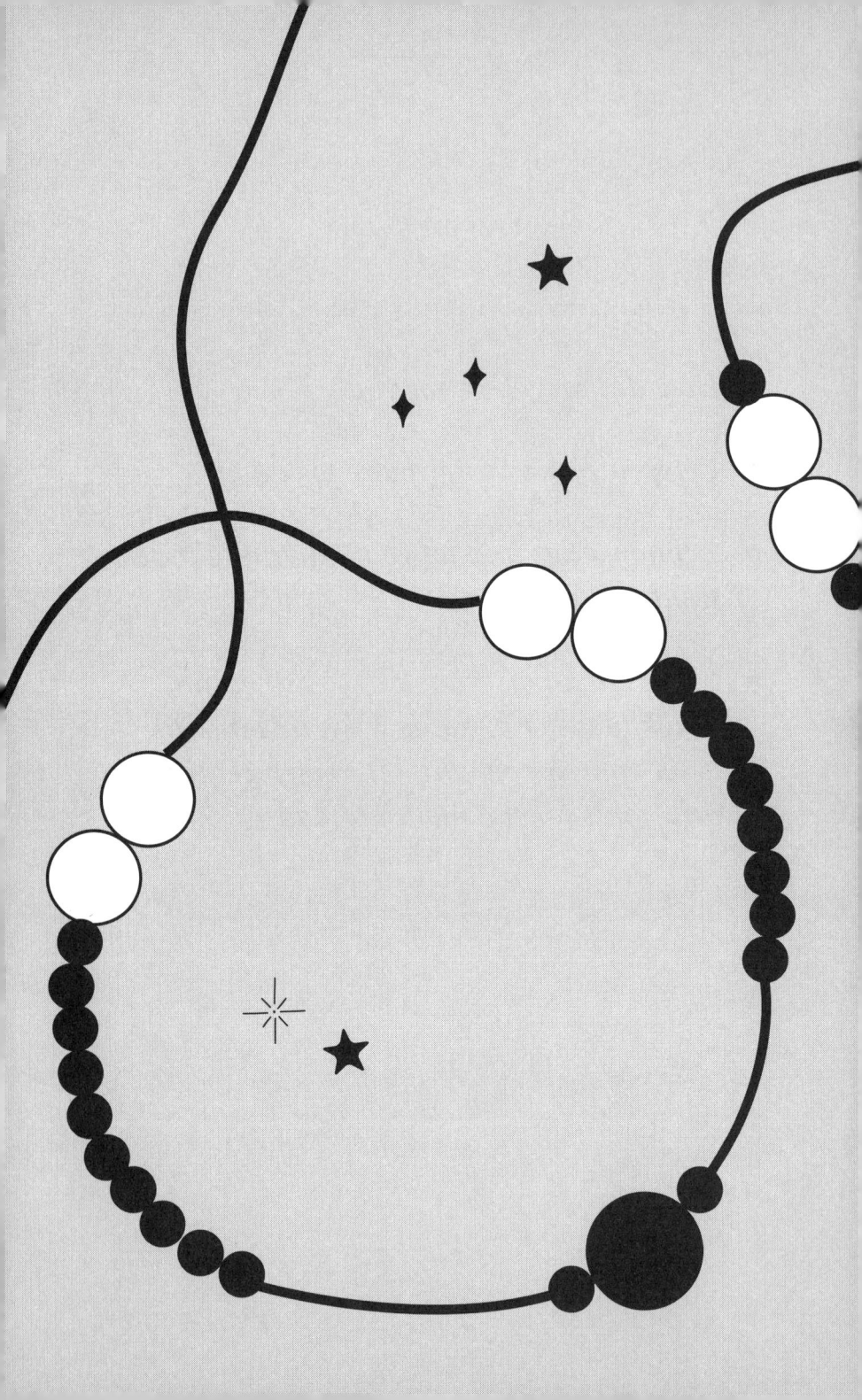

April

FEARLESS

Introduction

April is *Fearless*.

From running through green fields in the "Love Story" music video to dancing in a storm in "Fearless," this is a heady, joyful album, full of hope and earnest emotions. It's fully fledged romanticism and impulsiveness and dreaming. It's princess dresses and big, wild hair. It's anger and frustration aimed at the things you want not arriving yet. It's feeling both heartbroken and inspired by change. It's April.

This April, allow yourself to fully feel your feelings and not be ashamed of them. Rediscover things that bring you joy. It's a hopeful month, with summer just around the corner, and *Fearless* is a hopeful album. With a sense of renewed optimism and innocence, April is also a great moment to reconnect with a childlike sense of joy.

April means new beginnings. The name of the month itself comes from the Latin *aperire*, which means *to open*, and if you take a walk outside in the spring you'll see blossoms opening up on the trees. That makes *Fearless* the perfect album to soundtrack this month, inviting you to lean into the new and be open to the world around you.

As Taylor wrote in her original liner notes to the album, "To me, fearless is having fears." April is the perfect month to do what excites you in the face of these fears. Take inspiration from the rapid rate of change in the natural world around you, in the often-unpredictable nature of April weather, and use this as a springboard for making your own shifts this month.

Even in the naivety and hope of *Fearless*, Taylor confronts an important truth: the knowledge that—for good or bad—"these things will change." This is the only real certainty we can have—everything else is just hopes and fears.

Dream as big as you want. Embrace the good and the bad. Find happiness in how "the street looks when it's just rained."

And be fearless.

Use this April to lean into joy, innocence, and naivety.

Challenge your fears. Try to see through them to what you might be able to gain on the other side of conquering them.

Return to and reclaim the things that make you feel most like yourself. Embrace anything and everything that makes you happy, whether that's in Taylor's music or elsewhere in your life.

Get outside into the ever-changing nature of the world and embrace uncertainty—the suddenness with which new birdsong starts and stops, or how fast and slow blossom falls. Use fairy tales, heartfelt songs, and strong emotions to dream as big as you can, and don't be afraid of falling.

April is all about fresh starts.

"What
you're
looking
for has

been here the whole time"

EMBRACING YOUR FEARS

Sometimes we feel so suffocated by doubts and insecurities that we can't even express them. We're afraid to look them in the eye and acknowledge what scares us. Without confronting our fears, we're forced to remain stuck where we are.

To achieve change and reach any goals, we have to be willing to wade through what's uncomfortable and be prepared for the possibility of whatever frightens us most, whether that's failure, rejection, shame, or embarrassment.

In this exercise, articulate what scares you. Then think about what these thoughts, put down on paper, open you up to.

What is stopping you from going after what you want?

If you had to go through
this scenario or experience these
feelings, but with the knowledge
you would get what you want
on the other side, would
you do it?

Open yourself up to your fears.
What's the worst that could
happen if it all goes wrong?
Now imagine: What if
it all goes right?

Fearless

For many Taylor Swift fans, *Fearless* is an extremely nostalgic album that contains some of the earliest songs that made Taylor famous, like "Love Story" and "You Belong with Me." It's filled with fairy tales, princesses, star-crossed lovers, and meant-to-be romance. As the album ages and Taylor's fans grow up with it, it also serves as a time capsule: for the moment a young country artist experienced global success for the first time, for the feelings of hope and impulsiveness that run through it, often so bright and golden they're hard to pin down.

Fearless stays as perennial and timeless as ever on every listen, even as Taylor matures beyond the young girl who wrote the songs. Throughout the album, she uses classic archetypes of romance to make her feelings and experiences resonate beyond herself: the high school clichés of cheerleaders and football teams in "You Belong with Me" and "Fifteen"; the princesses and magic of "White Horse" and "Today Was a Fairytale"; and, of course, references in "Love Story" to *Romeo and Juliet*.

As her first record-breaking album, it makes sense that *Fearless* is the first album Taylor chose for her re-recording project. Reflecting on the album in the prologue to *Taylor's Version*, she writes, "It was a real honor to get to be a teenager alongside you." This very idea is part of the ongoing appeal of *Fearless*: it is a chance to return to simpler feelings, to naivety, heartbreak and hope, slipping the emotions and themes on like clothes borrowed from an old friend.

We can't talk about *Fearless* without talking about "Love Story." Taking the narrative of Romeo and Juliet but giving them their happy ending (with a surprise proposal and approving parents) symbolizes what's so captivating about *Fearless*. Taking familiar stories and feelings and making them her own, Taylor is unabashed in her hope and romanticism.

Sometimes, just sometimes, we get a glimpse of the real experiences beneath the glittering facade. The same pebbles thrown at a window in "Love Story" resurface in the much more grounded "The Other Side of the Door." It's this alchemy—turning real life into make-believe—that *Fearless* returns to again and again.

To some people, "Love Story" might be the only Taylor Swift song they know. To her fans, it's nostalgic and joyful. It takes on new meaning when Taylor performs it live, and videos flood social media of fans getting engaged as a stadium full of friends, lovers, and families scream "knelt to the ground and pulled out a ring." It's a fairy tale that could never have happened—a happy ending tacked on to a tragedy, a daydream made into something concrete—beloved by the fans who sing it as loud as they can until it becomes real.

That's *Fearless*. It's full of contradictions, doubts, and lessons learned. It's a longing for something and the feeling of devastation as you lose it, but also the capacity to embrace the nostalgia and community that comes with opening yourself up to potential joy. Through Taylor's mythical princesses, castles, rescues, and forevers, the ideas of love, loss, and innocence can be returned to in their purest, most fleeting state each time we listen.

FAN FAVORITES

Some of the most recognizable fan favorite moments come from *Fearless*. Heart hands, the *"Fearless"* stomps, the "You Belong with Me" clap, the "Love Story" proposal, or just watching Taylor on stage with her guitar and the band that have been with her since she was a teenager—something in this era keeps fans returning at different stages of their life.

What elements of Taylor's music feel nostalgic to you? Whether it's screaming a bridge with your friends, or watching surprise songs on a grainy livestream, take time to reflect and enjoy.

What was the first song you remember liking? Listen to it now—does something different resonate this time?

What songs take you back most vividly to a specific moment or season of your life? What song do you think sums up the chapter you're in now?

Are there any songs that remind you of other people and relationships? More importantly, are there any that remind you of yourself?

"Never knew I could feel that much"

EMOTION TRACKER

Instead of a habit tracker this month, try tracking your emotions. Check in with yourself each day and use your notes to make sense of when certain feelings come up for you and why that might be.

Fill in the below and try to track how these emotions most often show up for you. Is it how many days this month you laughed? How many you cried? How many times you felt the need to hide something out of embarrassment?

Recognizing tangible patterns and behaviors in how we act out our feelings can help us understand them.

Happiness for me looks like . . .

1 ○	2 ○	3 ○	4 ○	5 ○	6 ○	7 ○
8 ○	9 ○	10 ○	11 ○	12 ○	13 ○	14 ○
15 ○	16 ○	17 ○	18 ○	19 ○	20 ○	21 ○
22 ○	23 ○	24 ○	25 ○	26 ○	27 ○	28 ○
29 ○	30 ○					

Tick each day if this emotion is showing up for you

How's it going each week?

....

....

....

....

....

Sadness for me looks like . . .

1 ○	2 ○	3 ○	4 ○	5 ○	6 ○	7 ○
8 ○	9 ○	10 ○	11 ○	12 ○	13 ○	14 ○
15 ○	16 ○	17 ○	18 ○	19 ○	20 ○	21 ○
22 ○	23 ○	24 ○	25 ○	26 ○	27 ○	28 ○
29 ○	30 ○					

Tick each day if this emotion is showing up for you

How's it going each week?

....

....

....

....

....

april 1–7 WEEK 1

DAY

DAY

DAY

DAY

DAY

NOTES

DAY

DAY

PRIORITIES

april 8–14 WEEK 2

13

DAY

DAY

DAY

DAY

DAY

NOTES

DAY

PRIORITIES

DAY

april 15–21 WEEK 3

DAY

DAY

DAY

DAY

DAY

NOTES

DAY

DAY

PRIORITIES

april 22-28 WEEK 4

13

DAY

DAY

DAY

DAY

DAY

NOTES

DAY

DAY

PRIORITIES

april 29–30 WEEK 5

DAY	NOTES

DAY	PRIORITIES

REFLECTIONS

"I'm not a princess, this ain't a fairytale"

Committing to big dreams means opening ourselves up to vulnerability and disappointment. In "White Horse," one of the saddest songs on *Fearless*, we see the growing maturity and hurt that sits beneath the optimism of the rest of the album.

We have to be open to disappointment in our lives too. Sometimes, the only way something good will happen is if we always acknowledge the possibility that it might go wrong.

Look back on this month of dreaming and feeling and fears.

What's gone wrong this month?

And is there a way you can let yourself be OK with it, while still maintaining hope?

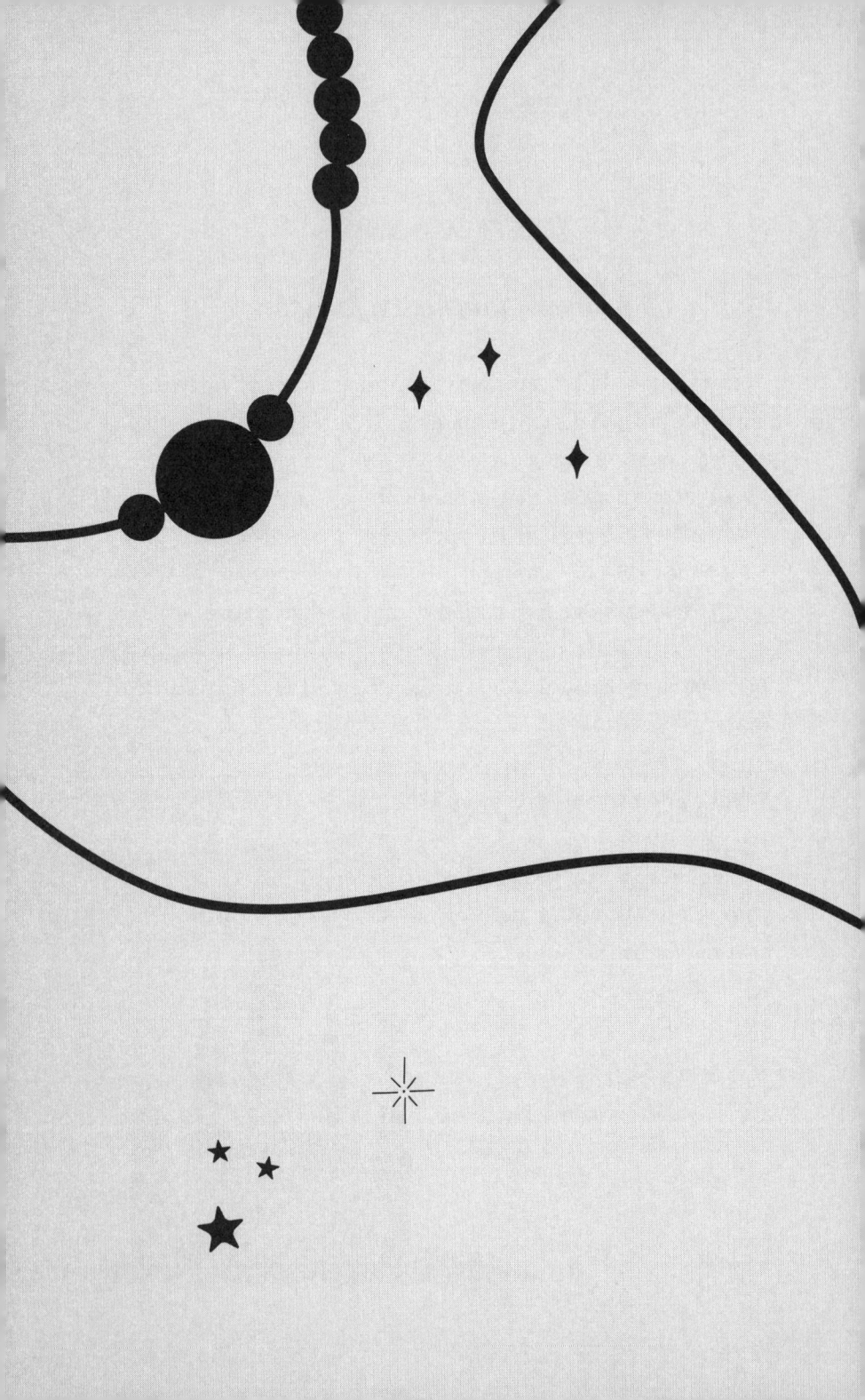

May

Introduction

May is *Taylor Swift*.

May is about growth and freedom. It's rolling green hills and days that get longer. It's butterflies and dragonflies skimming lazily over the water.

Summer is just around the corner, and with it all the memories and associations that summer brings: long school holidays, youthful recklessness, a warmth on your skin, and a feeling that, maybe, everything might just be OK.

May is a time to take long walks on your own as the evenings start to stretch out aimlessly before you. Spend time with just you and yourself, and be honest and vulnerable with your emotions.

From the lyrics about pick-up trucks and faded old jeans, to the blues, greens, and wild curly hair of the album cover, it's obvious that *Taylor Swift* is a summer album. But, as the self-titling suggests, it's an album that invites you to think about yourself at your most essential and most distilled. It's about finding yourself and defining who you are, and who you want to be. May is *Taylor Swift*.

Speaking in 2009 about the process of writing her first album, Taylor told the *Daily Telegraph*: "I genuinely felt that I was running out of time. I'd written all these songs and I wanted to capture these years of my life on an album while they still represented what I was going through."

It's a familiar, confusing feeling of youth: the knowledge that you have so much time left ahead of you running alongside a hunger to preserve what you have right now. The album captures the growing awareness that time is always slipping away. Use this May to get in touch with the core of who you are, what you want, and explore how you can preserve who you are now and what you're going through at this moment of your life.

May is a time to enjoy being stripped back and vulnerable. It's giddy, it's carefree, and sometimes it's unsure and confused. A transition between spring and summer, May is about letting yourself be. Think back on how far you've come this year and get excited about how far you still have to go.

Let the unknown excite you by remaining grounded in the fact that you always have yourself. This month can be your debut into a new phase, or it can be a moment of selfishness as you allow yourself to take time for yourself.

This is May.

This month, focus on discovering things about yourself. Establish what defines you with mood and vision board exercises. Keep diary entries to focus on what takes up your time and attention. Get in touch with younger versions of yourself, using the perspective you've since gained.

Spend time alone. Spend time laughing, wandering, and letting life take you where it decides to. Feel as uninhibited and searching as Taylor seems on the songs of her debut album, finding out where you sit in the world and what makes you *you*.

Enjoy the warmer weather and the brighter days, and don't worry about having it all figured out.

"Our song is the

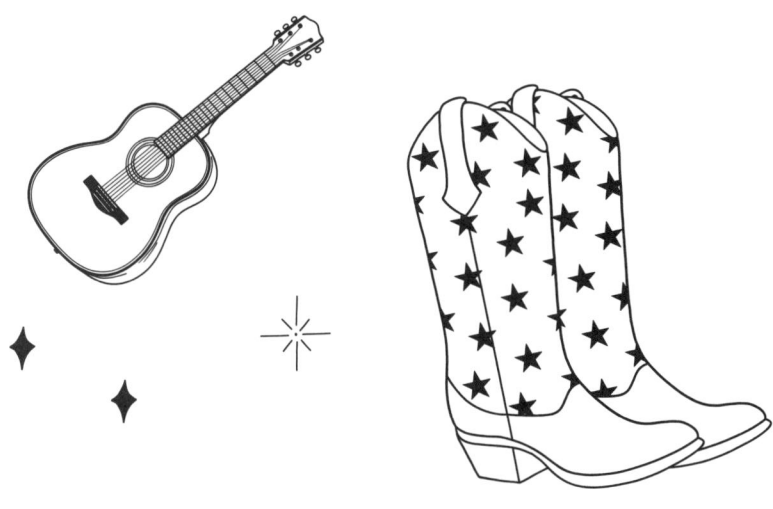

slamming screen door"

MOOD BOARDS

This month, curate your own life and aesthetic. With these mood board exercises, think about what you want to be associated with.

What makes people think about you? What makes you think most about yourself?

WHEN YOU THINK . . .

Start by listing anything you associate with yourself, as Taylor sings about on "Tim McGraw."

Get creative with your senses: what sounds, smells, feels, and tastes like home to you? Is there particular birdsong that reminds you summer is coming each year? Do you know the sound of a key turning in a lock without even realizing it? Is there a recipe or dish that feels nostalgic every time you eat it?

Are there songs, artists, styles, places, food, or drinks that you think remind people of you?

Get a big piece of paper or card and some photographs, magazines, scissors, and glue or tape (or create a virtual mood board). Start to place all the things that make you "you." If you're doing this by hand, you can add in doodles and glitter between the pictures.

OUR SONGS

Ask friends or family to send you the songs that remind them most of you, and add them to a playlist to create a musical mood board.

LIVING YOUR MOOD BOARD

Try to do one thing every day this month from your mood board, whether it's what you eat or a song you listen to. Do you feel more like yourself at the end of it?

Taylor Swift

Taylor's self-titled debut album announces itself with banjos, fiddles, and guitars, and a country twang that her voice has long since lost. Her teenage vocals are less polished than later in her career, but have a dreamy, inexperienced charm all of their own. Compared to the long career that's since followed, this is one of Taylor's more cohesive albums in its pure country style—unsurprising, given that in every album since, Taylor has always been eager to experiment and transition into new genres and styles of music.

Taylor Swift has an interesting, sometimes misunderstood place in her body of music. It can often be overlooked or simplified as the album before she became "Taylor Swift: the pop star." But that's precisely what makes it unique in her discography. In every album since, Taylor has had to carefully find ways to express her feelings and experiences outside of her own life, to pinpoint the details that make her songs accessible and relatable to all fans, despite the differences in situations. But in this album, we get a glimpse of Taylor Swift the teenager, rather than the singer.

We see her teenage angst with feisty, stompy singles like "Picture to Burn" and "Should've Said No." The strength with which Taylor has always stood up for herself is evident in songs like these, showing just a hint of the self-belief you'd need to chase a career as a singer at the tender age of thirteen.

Taylor Swift also has more lost and plaintive songs like "The Outside," about her experience of feeling left out at school—made all the more emotional by her uncertain, younger voice. When she sings in "The Outside" that she "would give it all up" to be included, parallels spring up with later song "You're on Your Own, Kid," a fan favorite from *Midnights* about embracing the truth that you can do things your own way. "Cold As You," meanwhile, shares startling lyricism for the age in which Taylor wrote it, where lines like "a mess of a dreamer with the nerve to adore you" would not be misplaced on her later albums like *folklore* and *evermore*.

In many ways, Taylor's debut album symbolizes mythology and archaeology to fans. All the strands of her personality—heartfelt, passionate, vulnerable—are there, long before it could ever be claimed that she crafted a character purely for her success. These are songs written before she ever thought the whole world was going to hear them.

This album also saw Taylor begin to establish the close relationships with fans that fostered the community she now has. Hidden messages could be found in the liner notes of *Taylor Swift* for fans to decode, a tradition she continued until *1989*. These two albums can be seen as bookends of the first stage of Taylor's fame and career. There are clear parallels with the titles compared to her other albums, which tend to focus on emotional states or thematic moods. *Taylor Swift* and *1989* are albums about her: her name and her year of birth. Each can be seen as Taylor introducing herself to the world, first as an aspiring young singer and then as a global megastar.

Now, the legacy of *Taylor Swift* is everywhere. During the Eras Tour, a debut set was missing, but her "surprise songs" acoustic section features a floral guitar in tribute to the one she first played. This most vulnerable and intimate of sets seems to be a nod to her most vulnerable and intimate of albums.

"So watch me strike a match on all my wasted time"

Lean into the young Taylor's angry performances of "Picture to Burn" and take some time this month to be destructive. Engaging with all our emotions includes unleashing the pettier, more impulsive side we might sometimes try to hide. Sometimes, we need to wallow in our feelings and act them out to let them go.

Write down a list of things you're unhappy about on a small piece of paper.

Don't spend time overanalyzing each entry, just note what creates the feeling of unhappiness.

Once done, tear the paper up.

Put the angriest Taylor Swift song on and sing as loud as you can.

A Place in This World

"I'll be strong, I'll be wrong"

Look back and look forward.

Halfway through this month, write a letter to your younger self from at least a year ago. Acknowledge the vulnerability and uncertainties you couldn't help having then, the mistakes you might have made, plus the things you're proud of yourself for.

At the end of the month, write a letter to your older self and visualize yourself a year from now. Have you found your place in the world? What might that look like?

Take stock and be introspective: what do you fear going wrong between then and now? What do you think life will be like—and what do you hope it will contain?

NATURE DIARY

May is the perfect month to listen to *Taylor Swift* and imagine yourself in the green hills and trees she sings about.

This month, try to spend some time outside each day and keep a record of your thoughts. If you find it difficult to journal, start by observing the nature around you in a garden, park, or just by looking out of the window. Set yourself a timer for five to ten minutes to write without stopping. You'll be surprised to see what pops up once you let your thoughts flow freely.

Try sitting in the same spot every day and focusing on how things around you change throughout the month. By the end of it, you might be able to trace how your inner state has changed.

What can you hear?

What can you smell?

What can you see?

How do you feel?

may 1–7 WEEK 1

DAY

DAY

DAY

DAY

DAY

NOTES

DAY

DAY

PRIORITIES

may 8-14 WEEK 2

DAY

DAY

DAY

DAY

DAY

NOTES

DAY

DAY

PRIORITIES

may 15–21 WEEK 3

DAY

DAY

DAY

DAY

DAY

NOTES

DAY

PRIORITIES

DAY

may 22–28 WEEK 4

DAY

DAY

DAY

DAY

DAY

NOTES

DAY

DAY

PRIORITIES

may **29–31** WEEK 5

DAY

DAY

DAY

NOTES

PRIORITIES

OVERVIEW

Here are some questions to reflect on at the end of this month:

★ *How did May go for you?*
  Celebrate one thing you're proud of.

★ *Acknowledge and let go of anything that went less well.*

★ *Set aside an afternoon to finish off any quick tasks or errands from this month, reset your space, and set your intentions and goals for the month ahead.*

June

LOVER

Introduction

June is *Lover*.

It's the start of summer, awash with pinks, pastels, and glowing gold. Toward the end of the month, we will experience the summer solstice—the longest day and shortest night of the year—promising light and joy.

The clue is in the title. *Lover* is an album that celebrates love in all its forms, and calls on listeners to romanticize their own lives and be courageous in their search for joy. It's as brave as it is vulnerable, as peaceful as it is palpably anxious.

It's the perfect album for the longest day and shortest night. It's the album that embodies the first warm, solid ray of sun of the year: June is *Lover*.

As aesthetic changes between eras go, the flip from *reputation* to *Lover* couldn't have been much stronger. Dark becomes light; revenge becomes the gleeful flippancy of "I Forgot That You Existed." The intimacy and vulnerability that run like a thread of silver through *reputation* emerge here into something stronger and deeper. It's glimmering still, but golden.

This month, like Taylor, take the brave step of being gentler and more heartfelt. Lean into what you love, and try to learn to be OK with the potential of being hurt. June is a month to pull what's close to you nearer still, to admire it out loud, and to live with gratitude and courage. Around the world Pride Month is celebrated in June, so celebrate and enjoy that feeling of pride and togetherness that Taylor pays homage to in the colorful music video for "You Need to Calm Down."

Channel something from *Lover* every day this month: whether that's practicing gratitude, doing something that brings you joy, spending time with loved ones, or just wearing your most colorful clothes.

Though love and affection coat every lyric and wedding-style marching melody of *Lover*, it is an album that feels both unchangeable and unpredictable. Taylor sings about love with conviction and tenderness, but never complacency. There's an anxious, too-good-to-be-true undercurrent strumming beneath every declaration of romance. Rather than being ashamed of your fears or insecurities this month, embrace them, dig into them, and try to be the keeper of your own happiness.

In June, the brightness of the summer solstice daylight is followed only by increasing darkness. Living with love, happiness, and joy is always a gamble. That's why taking the risk matters.

This June, let light into your life in whatever way you can.
Stay up all night at the summer solstice.

Practice gratitude for yourself, your life, and the people you love.

Check in on yourself and your goals halfway through the year, and meet any doubts or mistakes with compassion. Allow yourself to be scared, and to do the things that scare you anyway.

Let June be soft, golden, and gentle. Trust yourself and your happiness.

"Devils roll the dice,

angels roll
their eyes"

Summer Solstice

Summer solstice: the day with the longest period of daylight and shortest night of the year. At the North Pole, continuous daylight floods frozen oceans.

There's something giddy and euphoric about feeling like you're at the high point of the year. The traditional solstice celebrations of bonfires, feasting, and dancing are both undercut and made stronger—more vital—by the knowledge that the nights will only get longer after this. The days will be shorter, the dark times darker.

There's a similar energy to *Lover*. If this is happiness and peace, found and treasured at last, then what could possibly come next? If it can't get better than this, does that mean it's going to get worse? The key is in savoring joy where you find it, rather than worrying about whether it will last.

This summer solstice, practice gratitude for what you have and acknowledge any fears you may hold about eventually losing it.

SUMMER SOLSTICE ACTIVITIES

Sun Salutations
Stay up over the longest night and practice sun salutations with the sunrise.

Gratitude Journaling
Sit outside, soak up the sun, and practice gratitude without fear of loss. Acknowledge that change is always possible and let go of worrying about it.

Flower Crown Creation
Popular in many countries, use the traditional language of flowers to make a flower crown on the summer solstice, when plants and herbs are said to have more powerful effects:

Love—*roses*
Persistence—*gladioli*
Protection—*delphinium*

Lover

Sandwiched between the big, bold musical statement (and loud *lack* of public statement) of *reputation*, and the pivot to woodsy, alternative music with surprise pandemic album *folklore*, *Lover* in some ways seems like a temporary callback to the albums Taylor made her name with. It is full of love songs and pure pop music, and leans into the bubblegum, girly aesthetic her previous albums were often landed with in public perception.

But *Lover* shouldn't be dismissed as just a resting place, or a re-gathering of strength before Taylor embarked on new directions. Lyrically, it spans a broad and very vulnerable range of subjects, from confronting illness and mortality in "Soon You'll Get Better," to making her first political statements through song with "You Need to Calm Down" and "The Man."

While *Lover* is replete with love songs, track five—known to fans as Taylor's most vulnerable track on each album—is "The Archer," where her search for love and acceptance is symbolized by lyrical references to combat and a frustrating build-up of anxiety with no final release. In "Afterglow," she digs deeper into her own flaws, sowing the seeds for the more self-critical lyrics that would later pop up in *Midnights* and *The Tortured Poets Department* but still helplessly begging the song's subject to "tell me that it's not my fault."

These two contrasting sides to love—peace and fear—are perhaps best summed up on "Cornelia Street," which is both a loving recollection of "sacred new beginnings" and a kind of spell to ward off a relationship's foreseen end.

It seems that after *reputation*, the drama that preceded its release and the need to respond with a new attitude to the media and her public persona, Taylor found in *Lover* an ability to be wholly vulnerable and personal once more.

Lover is many things. It's a reclaiming of the kind of big-hearted, personal, romantic music that critics had accused Taylor of rehashing, and a diversion from the stormy path of *reputation* before it. It's an ode to the strongest, most secure love Taylor had ever felt in her life. It's also a record of the doubts and anxiety that spring up around this love. It's gentle, soft, and seductive, and at the same time poppy and upbeat.

It's the first album, you could say, where Taylor really owns her self.

Goals

Checking In

Halfway through the year, it's time to check in again with how you feel about your goals from January and March (see pages 10–11 and 54–55).

How Do You Feel About Your Goals Now?

At the halfway point of the year, it can be easy to slip into a state of anxiety about the time you have left to achieve your goals. Pay attention to any feelings that come up, including worries of time pressure, a lack of control or self-doubt.

GOAL 1: NOURISH WHAT YOU HAVE

....

....

....

....

....

....

....

....

GOAL 2: LEARN AND DEVELOP

....

....

....

....

....

....

....

....

GOAL 3: RECLAIM YOUR POWER

....

....

....

....

....

....

....

....

Now, try these visualization exercises to help you stop feeling stuck in these emotions.

"I see right through me"

In "The Archer," Taylor sings about feelings of exposure, imposter syndrome, and repeating negative patterns. Look within for a fundamental fear you have. Maybe it's a fear of being "found out," not being good enough, or repeating mistakes.

Sometimes, fears like these can be so central to our sense of worth they become debilitating, and we imagine them screaming out for the whole world to notice. Indulge this for just a moment—imagine yourself invisible, but with this fear or insecurity exposed and visible. Now, flip the narrative and imagine the thing you're most proud of yourself for. Perhaps it's a challenge you overcame, or a quality you know you have. What if that's what people can see right through you to? What if you saw it in yourself?

"I ask the traffic lights if it will be alright"

It can be hard to relinquish control of outcomes, particularly for something we really care about or have worked hard to achieve. Is there something on your mind this month that has you fixated on what you can't control?

Take a moment to visualize, as Taylor sings about in "Death by a Thousand Cuts," a traffic light flowing from red, yellow, to green again. Recognize that everything is up to chance, and the only thing within our control is our own behavior.

Whatever you want to achieve, try to imagine that the light could be red or could be green—the only thing you can do is wait and see which one appears for you.

"This is our place, we make the rules"

One of the healthiest ways to deal with anxiety is to set boundaries to protect your space, both physical and emotional. This month, think about what makes you feel safe, grounded, and in control. It can be difficult to set boundaries, particularly with people that we're close to, but it's a habit that can only get easier through practice.

Physical Boundary: My Place

Is there a level of privacy that you need to feel peaceful at home? In shared spaces, can you establish the cleanliness or organization that you feel most comfortable with? Practice setting these boundaries.

Emotional Boundary: My Rules

Whether an emotional boundary for you is taking the time you need to reply to messages properly, not being around certain people that you find uncomfortable or doing or activities you don't want to— sometimes it's OK to reset expectations of what you will or won't do.

"I want to be defined by the things that I love"

Lover is all about choosing joy and happiness over fear or insecurity. Answer these questions to help define yourself in positive ways only.

Who do you love most in this world?

Which place makes you happiest?

What memory is most precious to you?

What hobby or activity brings you the most joy?

Imagine a weekend, or day, or even a few hours, solely dedicated to what you love. Where would you be and who would you be there with? It could be time with those close to you, or time alone doing something important to you, but try to find some time this month to be wholly defined and motivated by what you love.

june 1-7 WEEK 1

DAY

DAY

DAY

DAY

DAY

NOTES

DAY

DAY

PRIORITIES

june 8–14 WEEK 2

DAY

DAY

DAY

DAY

DAY

NOTES

DAY

PRIORITIES

DAY

june 15–21 WEEK 3

DAY

DAY

DAY

DAY

DAY

NOTES

DAY

DAY

PRIORITIES

june 22-28 WEEK 4

DAY

DAY

DAY

DAY

DAY

NOTES

DAY

DAY

PRIORITIES

june 29-30 WEEK 5

DAY

NOTES

DAY

PRIORITIES

OVERVIEW

Here are some questions to reflect on at the end of this month:

★ *How did June go for you?*

★ *Celebrate one thing you're proud of.*

★ *Acknowledge and let go of anything that went less well.*

★ *Set aside an afternoon to finish off any quick tasks or errands from this month, reset your space, and set your intentions and goals for the month ahead.*

Introduction

July is *1989*.

It's the height of summer. Think blue skies, trips to the beach, and seagulls dipping and soaring overhead.

Imagine sand between your toes. Laughing with friends until your stomach hurts. Walking in a new city alone and feeling brave enough to be by yourself.

July is a time for freedom, creating memories, and trying new things. Taking risks and making mistakes are all part of the process.

From the New York City skyline that dominated much of the original 2014 release's aesthetic, to the beachy vibes of *Taylor's Version*, *1989* is the epitome of a summer album. But it's also as much about being alone and finding yourself as it is about having fun with your friends. It makes you feel loneliness and contemplation, as well as joy and spontaneity.

This is an album all about defining the moment and reinventing yourself. It feels tightly packed and warm and energetic, like one chaotic, busy summer in the city. It's so defined not just by place, but by Taylor's state of mind at the time—her independence, her rejection of criticism, her decision to shake off pain instead of letting it wound her—that the album can't be extracted from it. Lean into this mood in July and define the month for yourself in absolutes. Try on new personalities like they'll be yours forever, and discard them with ease.

1989 is boats racing across the blue ocean and summer nights in a new place. It's blurred polaroids and Taylor's Fourth of July parties. It's fireworks, vintage sunglasses, and maybe bringing a sweater to that beach trip because it might be colder than you think. It's being out on the sand, the wind biting into you, and feeling fresh, clean, and more alive than ever.

This July, put yourself first and lean into new experiences and learnings about yourself.

There's a place in our lives to be selfish, and this July might just be it for you. Not everything has to be serious or has to go right for us to learn from our mistakes. The most important thing is putting yourself first and growing.

Take just one day in July to do exactly what you want, and act like the person you want to be—and see how powerful this makes you feel.

Curate who you want to be, and make sure to leave room for fun and impulsiveness. Learn to laugh at yourself and not take other people's opinions of you too seriously.

Let go of what makes you feel uncertain and allow yourself to run toward fun and freedom.

"The best people

*in life
are
free"*

Defining Yourself

Use *1989* as your inspiration to define yourself and who you want to be. On the album, a lot of the power in Taylor's self-expression and reinvention comes from where she is and who she spends time with. While you may not be able to drop everything and move to a brand-new city, make a whole new group of friends, or throw a huge Fourth of July party, carve out some time this month to be intentional.

Activity: A Day for You

Take some time to plan out a day that makes you feel like the ideal version of "you"—with no detail too small. Ideally, try and find a day with no other plans.

What time do you wake up?
What do you wear?
Do you see friends, or spend time alone?
What music soundtracks this day?
Where do you go to feel the most "you"?

A DAY FOR YOU

6:00	TO DO
7:00	
8:00	
9:00	
10:00	
11:00	
12:00	
1:00	
2:00	
3:00	SHOPPING LIST
4:00	
5:00	
6:00	
7:00	
8:00	
9:00	
10:00	
11:00	

1989

1989's opener, "Welcome to New York," sets the stage for this album as cleanly as the opening shot of a film. This is far away from the diaristic hyper-specificity—the pinprick detailing of intimate moments that make you feel like you're right there with her—that define *Fearless* and *Speak Now*, and peaked with her previous album, *Red*.

We're in a cityscape, vast and deliciously anonymous, the crisp rhythm of synths rising like sharp skyscrapers. While there is the real-life precision of place, it's lacking the street-specific details of a real New York address, "Cornelia Street," on her follow-up album *reputation*. You can feel Taylor's mischievous delight as she sings: "Took our broken hearts, put them in a drawer." The message is clear: this is not an album of introspection and reflection. This is an album about coming up for air and reinventing yourself.

There's a satisfactory full circle to an album all about being alone in a big city, following up from the younger Taylor's promise to her detractors in *Speak Now*'s "Mean": "Someday I'll be living in a big old city." Success is here for Taylor on the most absolute, global scale, and it's as bright and blinding as the city lights she sings about. Beneath the slick pop of *1989*'s production, there's an enjoyable spikiness as Taylor leans for the first time into self-reliance, confidence and independence. Sometimes—as with one of the biggest songs on the album's release, "Blank Space"—this tips into a knowing caricature of how the media often portrays her.

This is the height of Taylor's self-possession of her own image, soon to be followed—with *reputation* and the drama around the ownership of her masters—by an abrupt reckoning with reality: we can't control what others think of us. Laughing at it won't actually lessen the pain it might cause. But here we can revel with Taylor in the freedom of reinvention, the feeling of blissful autonomy.

1989 does have a more vulnerable side to it, usually symbolized by a change of scene: the woods, the water, even just a private moment inside an apartment. "You Are in Love" returns to the intimacy of "burnt toast, Sunday" interior scenes often found on *Red* or *Speak Now*. These moments of romantic hope are intensified in the "From the Vault" tracks, most notably "Slut," with its dreamy sound and "moonlight swimming pools." But these are only temporary escapes—signified by the exit from the kaleidoscopic grid of the city streets—and Taylor always returns to the process of claiming and reinventing herself.

In the prologue of the re-recording, she reflects on this period of her life, writing: "I was born in 1989, reinvented for the first time in 2014, and a part of me was reclaimed in 2023 with the re-release of this album I love so dearly." Gone is the cheerfully naive belief that we can reinvent ourselves wholly; now Taylor recognizes that we can only define ourselves in bits and pieces. Reflecting on this season of huge change and reinvention, it's clear that Taylor feels proud of her younger self precisely for the optimism of her belief—in the power of moving to a new city, finding new friends, and becoming a new version of herself.

A New Chapter

We're now in the second half of the year. It's a great time to use *1989* to prompt you to start afresh or make a change in whichever part of your life you think needs it. This could be a personal goal, a new project, or just a fresh perspective or attitude.

A New Chapter Plan

Break down your vision of change for a new chapter into actionable steps. Set a specific goal for each month for the rest of this year to help turn your new chapter into reality. On the next page, we'll dive into your July goal, which will focus on new routines.

JULY

....

AUGUST

....

SEPTEMBER

....

OCTOBER

....

NOVEMBER

....

DECEMBER

....

New Routines

As Taylor sings about in "Clean," there's something incredibly symbolic and powerful at the thought of washing away and cleansing the stress of a situation or negative experience.

This month, think of a new routine you can introduce at the start or the end of the day. It can be something physical or mental—but it should feel like a fresh start, and carry a sense of renewal, whether to carry you into a new day or get you ready for the next one.

If you're stuck on ideas, make it as literal as possible: add a step of washing your face, or clearing away something in your room. Then try adding a mental component to it: are there affirmations you can say to yourself in the mirror, or write on a note after you've tidied your space?

july 1–7 WEEK 1

DAY

DAY

DAY

DAY

DAY

NOTES

DAY

DAY

PRIORITIES

july 8-14 WEEK 2

DAY

DAY

DAY

DAY

DAY

DAY

NOTES

DAY

PRIORITIES

july 15–21 WEEK 3

DAY

DAY

DAY

DAY

DAY

NOTES

DAY

DAY

PRIORITIES

DAY

DAY

DAY

DAY

DAY

NOTES

DAY

DAY

PRIORITIES

july 29–31 WEEK 5

DAY

DAY

DAY

NOTES

PRIORITIES

REFLECTIONS

"The monsters turned out to be just trees"

Part of the joy of *1989* is being OK with making mistakes, and opening yourself up to change—in your opinion, your perception and your understanding of the world around you.

It's OK to have gotten things wrong, or to have misunderstood what was in front of you. Can you think of something you misunderstood, and see differently in hindsight? Extend understanding to that past version of yourself.

"Was it over then? And is it over now?"

"Out of the Woods" and "Is It Over Now?" play out an interesting dialogue about a situation that never feels quite "done," as although written at the same time, they were released almost a decade apart.

"Is It Over Now?" delves deeper into the uncertainty and specificity of the situation than "Out of the Woods" did, with its lingering questions in the original 2014 release of the album.

It's OK to have never gotten closure from situations—a messy ending can still be an ending. Challenge yourself to think of the furthest away memory you still feel unsure about. If you can find old diary entries from that time, great, or just try to recall it as closely as you can. How do you feel about it now?

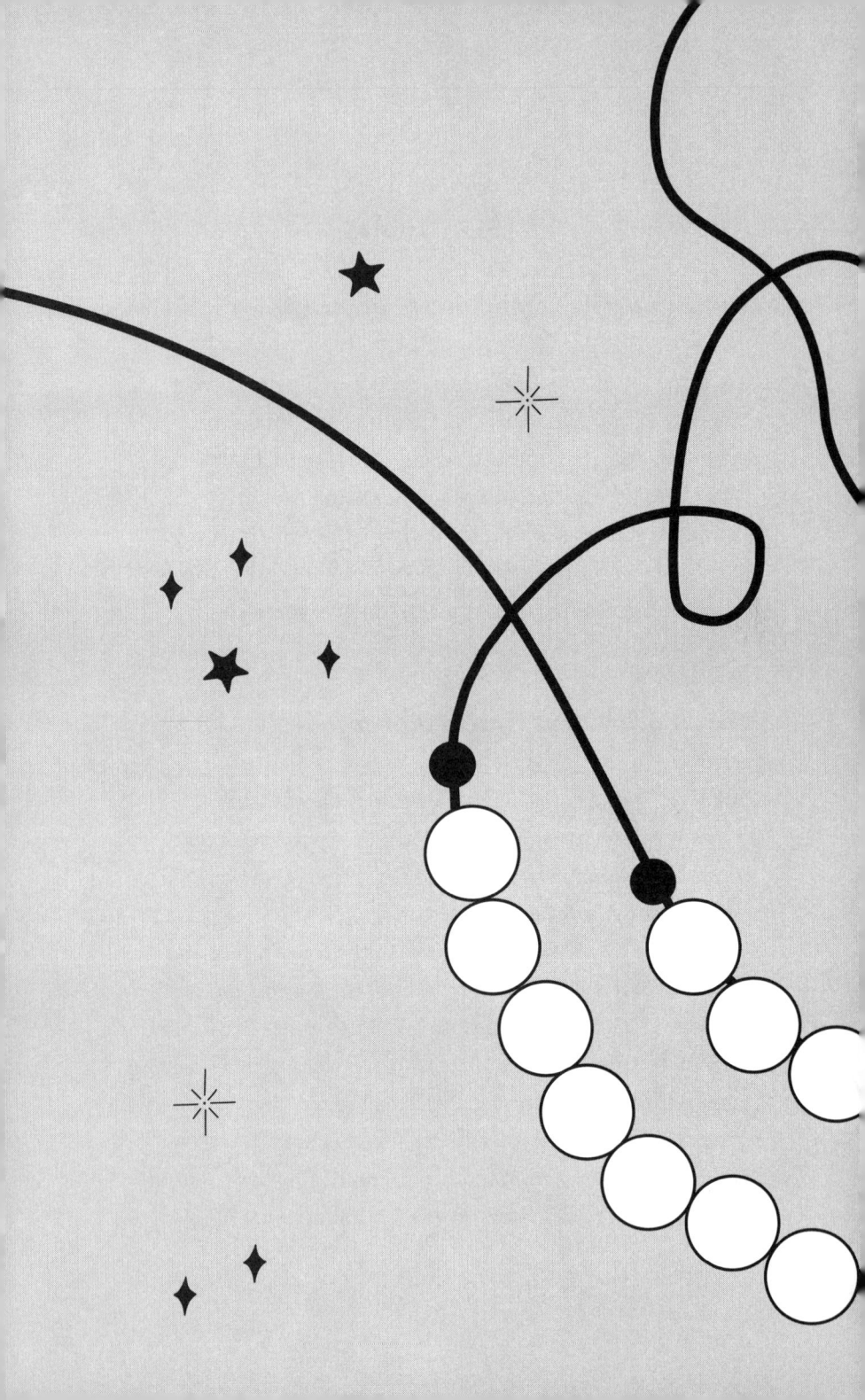

Introduction

August is *folklore*.

That end-of-summer feeling starts to sink in. Perhaps the heat starts to lessen, perhaps the slightly shorter evenings push you toward introspection. It's a time for reflection and wistfulness. It's the perfect time for *folklore*.

After the peak of summer, you might find yourself winding down and craving time alone. August is a perfect month to look back at what may have been a busy summer for you.

In *folklore*, Taylor surprised her fans not just with the unexpected release, but also with the change of sound: a new indie-folk style, featuring lots of acoustic guitars and stripped-back production. It sounds like the end of summer, soothing and cozy in August's fading golden sunlight.

folklore was released in the midst of the COVID-19 pandemic, and provides a sense of low-key comfort and soothing escapism that was perfect for what was a difficult, anxiety-inducing time for many. It makes sense to return to *folklore* in transitional seasons, such as the end of summer. If you're someone who finds the end of summer and the return of the darker, colder months hard, allow yourself to escape into the lost worlds and narrative storytelling of *folklore*.

Summer's nearly over, and it can feel like an age of gray now stretches before you until the sunshine will return next year. Use this August to lean into this sometimes unavoidable feeling of lost chances and what-ifs. Songs on *folklore* like "the 1" explore this longing for something we never had. Sometimes we need space for reflection, nostalgia, wistfulness.

Not every month can be about forging ahead. Sometimes we need to wander through the grass and feel the dew cooling.

This August, sit with your feelings, your regrets, your wonderings. As a new season peeks through in the changing leaves and cooling air, don't be afraid to slow down and wander through stories and memories.

By the end of this month, the air will be cooler, and September will be around the corner, bringing with it the sense of a "second new year," another fresh start. This August, spend time in the here and now, and even allow yourself some trips into the past.

Reflect on things that perhaps didn't go to plan—and acknowledge that we can still feel a loss for something we never had.

Revisit summers long in the past and remember the things you used to love then. Use the rich storytelling of *folklore* to reflect on memories, and try to understand things from different perspectives.

Encourage yourself to find stillness and peace, rather than trying to adapt to and entertain everyone around you. Get lost in nature, if you can, and make lots of time for solo walks as the warm weather starts to come to an end.

"August slipped away into

a moment in time"

END-OF-SUMMER REFLECTIONS

Now that the season is slipping away, it's a good time to reflect on the summer you've had and release anything you need to let go of.

As Taylor sings about in "the 1," sometimes it seems like: "The greatest films of all time were never made."

Reflect on a moment this summer where you wonder whether things could have gone differently.

How do you feel about it now?

What lessons can you learn from this experience?

"I'm still on that tightrope"

The business of summer can be all go, and can make you feel like you're trying to be everything to everyone. Carve out space this month to rest and be there only for yourself. How does it feel to get off that tightrope, and stop trying to reflect everything around you?

This could look like:

Changing up an established routine that people expect of you, and letting them know you'll no longer be doing that.

Adding in ten to fifteen minutes at the start or end of each day to do something only for yourself.

Practicing saying no when you're in the habit of always saying yes.

folklore

Released out of nowhere in 2020, in the middle of the COVID-19 pandemic, *folklore* is like a gasp of cool water at the end of a hot summer, or a lonely walk through the woods after a season of busy activity. It's mellow, sometimes melancholy, but also nostalgic and comforting.

folklore heralded a shift of style with its acoustic instruments and minimalistic production, but these changes were nothing new to Taylor, who has innovated at many junctures of her career in terms of sound. What set *folklore* apart and signified a real movement in Taylor's artistry was the songwriting.

folklore is—as the name suggests—a richly braided world of storytelling, where Taylor moves beyond personal, diaristic songwriting to explore fictional narratives. It's filled with character studies, intricately developed histories, and even multiple songs about the same characters and events from different perspectives, making this perhaps her most cohesive and immersive album yet. With songs "betty," "cardigan," and "august," Taylor draws us into a high-school love triangle perfect for the fading days of summer. Using these multiple perspectives—something she'd rarely explored before with her personal songwriting—enables Taylor to lean more fully into *folklore*'s themes of nostalgia, regret, and the passage of time, sitting comfortably within the rights and wrongs, victories and losses, of each member of her trio.

Woven into the deeply developed storytelling, however, are a few nods to Taylor's own life at the time. In a locked-down landscape that felt incredibly isolating to many people, and in a deeply private personal relationship, it makes sense that this was a period of time where Taylor's personal life was at its most mysterious. Taylor revealed in her *Folklore: The Long Pond Studio Sessions* documentary that "mirrorball" was written after her Lover Fest tour was canceled due to COVID-19, while *folklore*'s track five, "my tears ricochet," once again acts as a marker for Taylor's most personal feelings at the time of writing.

In the woodsy, folksy world of the album, "my tears ricochet" stands out with haunting, alien-sounding backing vocals and subtle, anxious drums and synths rising and falling in the background. It feels like a barren nightmare version of the gentle woods in which most of the album seems to be set, and lyrically nods toward feelings of betrayal that many have been linked to Taylor's masters dispute. With lines like "I can go anywhere I want, just not home," it also nods toward the purpose of *folklore*'s alternative storytelling methods. In a time of both personal and global uncertainty, Taylor delved into the fairy-tale worlds of others—and brought her fans much-needed comfort and release from their own struggles.

STORYTELLING

Through three different songs on *folklore*, Taylor moves through the perspectives of three people who loved, hurt and lost each other. Storytelling and imagining yourself in different perspectives can be a really useful way of making sense of your feelings and experiences. Use these two prompts from "cardigan" and "betty"—songs narrated by two characters, Betty and James, on opposing sides of a moment of betrayal—to examine your own perspectives and the experiences of others.

"I knew everything when I was young"

Reflect on a time when you felt certain of something that has since ended or changed. How does it feel to acknowledge that your feelings are different now?

"I'm only 17, I don't know anything"

With what you know now about this situation, can you reflect on the actions of anyone else who was involved? By recognising your own naivety or limited perspective, can you have more empathy for the limitations of others?

"Would it be enough if I could never give you peace?"

Try to find some time this month to give yourself small moments of absolute peace and stillness. It can feel counterintuitive to lean into rest instead of movement and action, and peace can never be guaranteed. But, even in seasons of change, it can be really restorative to sit with yourself.

This month, try to find a way to "watch wisteria grow right over [your] bare feet," as Taylor sings about in "the lakes." Take time in nature, and sit still—with no music or podcast, no book or journal—to just watch the world around you.

Give yourself peace, and acknowledge that this kind of stillness and rest is as necessary as it is temporary.

How does it feel to just be with yourself?

Childhood Summers

In the nostalgic song "seven," Taylor imagines herself looking back on the summers of a child and their best friend. How much can you remember from summers when you were younger?

Perhaps the days felt endless, the long weeks of vacation sometimes dull and boring, other times packed with excitement. Perhaps there was someone you spent a lot of time with, or perhaps you remember mainly being alone.

Try one of these activities to bring some of that childlike innocence into your own summer:

Visit somewhere familiar from summers in the past. How has it changed from your memory? Perhaps something that once seemed vast is now surprisingly small?

Return to an activity—like a craft or a sport, or even a favorite book—that you loved when you were younger.

Find a photograph of yourself when you were younger, and spend time picturing that version of yourself. Write a letter to your younger self about what your life was like then, and how it is now.

"And though I can't recall your face . . ."

august 1-7 WEEK 1

DAY

DAY

DAY

DAY

DAY

NOTES

DAY

DAY

PRIORITIES

august 8-14 WEEK 2

DAY

DAY

DAY

DAY

DAY

NOTES

DAY

DAY

PRIORITIES

august 15–21 WEEK 3

DAY

DAY

DAY

DAY

DAY

NOTES

DAY

DAY

PRIORITIES

august **22–28** WEEK 4

DAY

DAY

DAY

DAY

DAY

NOTES

DAY

PRIORITIES

DAY

august 29–31 WEEK 5

DAY

DAY

DAY

NOTES

PRIORITIES

OVERVIEW

Here are some questions to reflect on at the end of this month:

★ *How did August go for you?*

★ *Celebrate one thing you're proud of.*

★ *Acknowledge and let go of anything that went less well.*

★ *Set aside an afternoon to finish off any quick tasks or errands from this month, reset your space, and set your intentions and goals for the month ahead.*

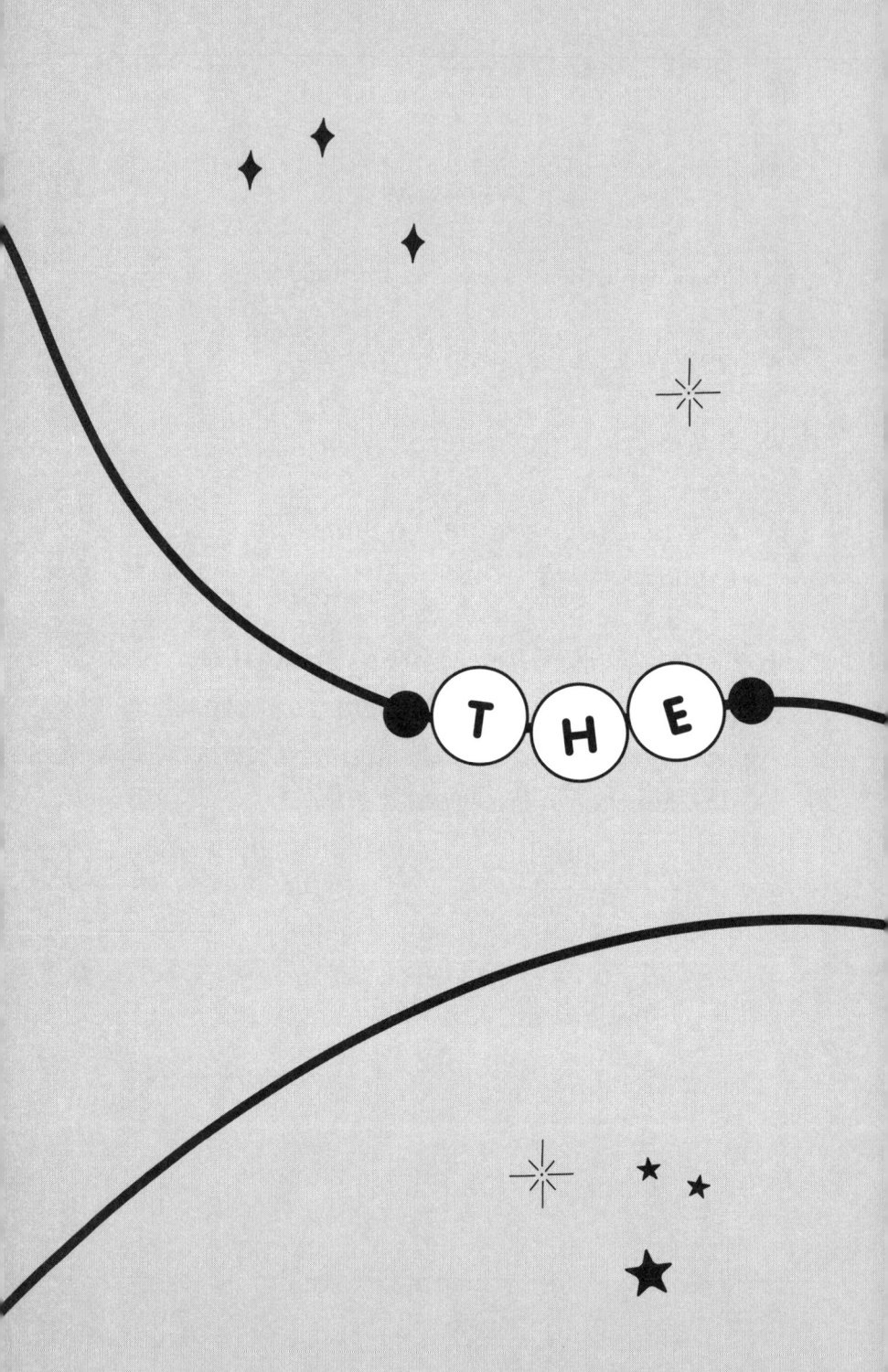

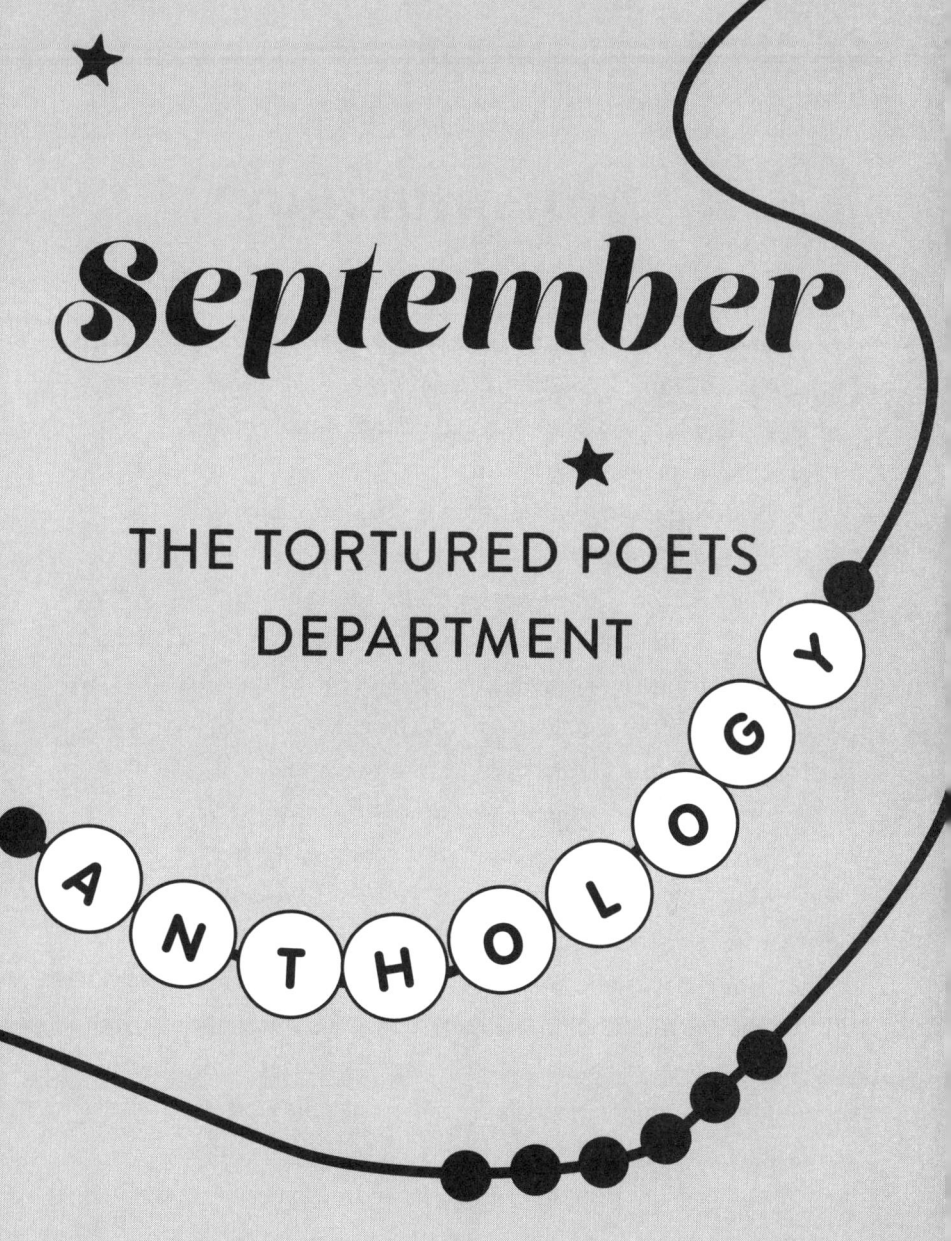

September

★

THE TORTURED POETS DEPARTMENT

ANTHOLOGY

Introduction

September is *The Tortured Poets Department: The Anthology*.
At the end of summer—after the heat receding, the late-summer storms, the muggy descent of the days into darker nights—September is a cool breath of air.

And, after the raw, dark, often heartbreaking turmoil of *The Tortured Poets Department*, there's something fresh in the album's second chapter, *The Anthology*—dropped as a surprise double album in 2024. Though there's just as much melancholy and anger, it feels more mellow and less overwhelming than the album's first part, with Taylor seeming more able to cope with her heavy emotions. Scattered through these songs—like bright autumn leaves starting to drift down in September—there's newness, and there's hope.

Wherever you are in life, for many people September is permanently tied to that back-to-school feeling. Last month we explored different perspectives with Taylor's high-school love triangle in *folklore*, and that feeling of wasted time, lost chances, and anticipation that can hit at the end of summer. This month, through songs like "So High School," "thanK you aIMee," and "Peter," we can lean fully into all the emotions that might come up this year, with the giddy fresh starts and stark disappointments that arise at transitional moments.

With the changing colors and fresher air, September is the perfect time to start anew—a second chance at the year. But with the cycling colors of the trees, and the suddenness with which the air turns cold and leaves start to fall, we can sometimes get locked into feelings of repetitiveness. It can be a melancholy month, as well as a hopeful one.

September is a transitional month: sometimes as warm and sunny—or even more so—than the summer months, other times immediately locking down into gray days and endless rain. We can choose to feel sad that summer is over for the year, or switch our perspective and lean into the anticipation of autumn and winter activities to come.

This thread—of hope, change, newness—isn't always easy to find through *The Anthology*, but it's there. Find that thread this September; let go of summer and get ready for the rest of the year.

Embrace September's bright, contradictory characteristics this month.

Lean into nostalgia and that back-to-school feeling with a trip down memory lane.

Watch the leaves start to turn red and gold, and use this transitional season as a moment to let go and move on. Allow change in and let negative experiences leave your life.

With this sense of renewal, be prepared for anxieties around growth, mistakes, and habits. Use a habit tracker to make concrete steps and reflect on your own internal narratives.

With the start of autumn, let September be many things at once—both a fresh beginning and a bittersweet ending.

"Old habits

habits

die screaming"

imgonnagetyouback

HABIT TRACKER

September can be a second chance at a fresh start to the year, so
return to January's habit tracker on pages 16–17 and see how you feel
about the habits there. Have you managed to incorporate any of them
into your routines? Are they still useful to your life and goals now?

Track three habits again this month—they can be the same as at
the start of the year, or something different—and notice whether, with
your growth over this year, sticking to habits comes easier to you now.

Habit 1

| 1 | 2 | 3 | 4 | 5 | 6 | 7 |
| ○ | ○ | ○ | ○ | ○ | ○ | ○ |

How's it going each week?

....

| 8 | 9 | 10 | 11 | 12 | 13 | 14 |
| ○ | ○ | ○ | ○ | ○ | ○ | ○ |

....

| 15 | 16 | 17 | 18 | 19 | 20 | 21 |
| ○ | ○ | ○ | ○ | ○ | ○ | ○ |

....

| 22 | 23 | 24 | 25 | 26 | 27 | 28 |
| ○ | ○ | ○ | ○ | ○ | ○ | ○ |

....

| 29 | 30 |
| ○ | ○ |

Tick each day when you
have completed your habit

....

Habit 2

1	2	3	4	5	6	7
○	○	○	○	○	○	○

8	9	10	11	12	13	14
○	○	○	○	○	○	○

15	16	17	18	19	20	21
○	○	○	○	○	○	○

22	23	24	25	26	27	28
○	○	○	○	○	○	○

29	30
○	○

Tick each day when you have completed your habit

How's it going each week?

....

....

....

....

....

Habit 3

1	2	3	4	5	6	7
○	○	○	○	○	○	○

8	9	10	11	12	13	14
○	○	○	○	○	○	○

15	16	17	18	19	20	21
○	○	○	○	○	○	○

22	23	24	25	26	27	28
○	○	○	○	○	○	○

29	30
○	○

Tick each day when you have completed your habit

How's it going each week?

....

....

....

....

The Tortured Poets Department: The Anthology

This surprise second part to *The Tortured Poets Department* explores many of the same themes—heartbreak, grief, anger, betrayal, freedom—but with an acoustic, folky sound that brings it closer to Taylor's earlier albums *folklore* and *evermore*.

With this softer, mellower sound, Taylor is able to explore the same big emotions in subtler ways, through character studies like "Peter" and "The Bolter," references to mythology, folklore, and storytelling, and self-reflection on her own flaws and growth.

Songs like "I Hate It Here" and "The Manuscript" combine fictional storytelling with references to both her past relationships and her songwriting processes, making them some of the most introspective songs in Taylor's whole discography. The "secret gardens in my mind" that Taylor escapes to in "I Hate It Here" seem to call back to the mythical woods she has described herself as "getting lost in" during the writing of *folklore* and *evermore*, perhaps hinting that she was drawn to craft other characters as an escape from her own pain. As with those albums, we get the sense with the fifteen extra songs here that Taylor was compelled to journey deeper into her experiences and ideas in the process of creating *The Tortured Poets Department*—in a sense, *The Anthology* is a sister album in much the same ways *evermore* is to *folklore*.

That's not to say, though, that *The Anthology* lacks the gut-punch emotional hits that the album's first part was full of. In songs like "Chloe or Sam or Sophia or Marcus," we feel the full force of Taylor's pain and frustration again, but with a further sense of restraint and even hopelessness: "And I just watched it happen," she sings quietly, seemingly unable to accept her own lack of action or autonomy in a painful situation. This more subdued heartbreak is at its most affecting in "How Did It End?"—acting as the famously vulnerable track five in this second part—where Taylor puzzles with aching uncertainty over how, exactly, it all went wrong.

No conclusive answers are gained. This isn't that kind of album—it's one that questions: How could they? How could I? Why did that happen?—without providing explanations. But when the two strands of songwriting on *The Anthology* are considered together—the direct explorations of heartbreak, and the more meandering fictional narratives and character studies—one clear thematic note emerges. "How Did It End?" features the line "Come one, come all, it's happening again"—and from songs like "The Albatross" through to "Cassandra" and "The Bolter," it's clear that Taylor is ruminating on patterns of pain and loss and betrayal, much more than just one heartbreak.

IDENTIFYING PATTERNS

Sometimes seasonal change can set us back into habits or mindsets we've outgrown. Use these prompts to consider aspects of your life you feel stuck in. Acknowledging these is the first step to being able to put negative feelings or behaviors to one side.

"And I tried to warn you about them"

Look up the legendary meaning of albatrosses or read the Samuel Taylor Coleridge poem of the same name while listening to "The Albatross." Perhaps there's some past experience you feel burdened by, or you worry that others might see you as a burden. As Taylor does in this song, try flipping your experience to reclaim your own power and autonomy. Sometimes "the albatross" can be the rescuer and the warner, rather than a symbol of bad luck or something to be avoided.

"You can mark my words I said it first"

Drawing from Greek mythology, Cassandra is a soothsayer cursed with never having any of her prophecies believed. Feeling distrusted or overlooked can be incredibly isolating, and can lead you to doubt your own instincts.

Having said that, leaning into this feeling of predicting bad outcomes can make us feel embittered and cynical toward the world. Can you feel surer of yourself and tune out the news of others by declaring your ambitions for something positive?

"Change the prophecy"

Is there a belief you repeat to yourself about something you'll never get—or maybe even deserve? Challenge yourself to write this belief down, and then write the opposite. Try to imagine what you want at the end of the prophecy, and reframe any struggles or roadblocks as tools to help you get there.

Fresh Starts and Forgiveness

"There wouldn't be this if there hadn't been you"

In this season of change, is there a painful moment in your past you can leave behind? Though it hurt you then, think about the growth you have had since.

Can you use positives gained from a bad experience to understand and forgive?

"Love's never lost when perspective is earned"

In "Peter," Taylor sings about letting go of someone from your past, using J. M. Barrie's "boy who never grew up" as a metaphor. It can be hard to process loss when, instead of closure, you have to accept and move on from a situation that isn't changing. But can you think about perspectives you've gained to transform your thinking from loss into growth?

"The brink of a wrinkle in time"

Embrace September's nostalgia and end the month with a positive walk down memory lane. Can you revisit something that reminds you of past Septembers?

It could be a physical walk to a familiar place, a phone call with someone from your past, looking at old pictures, or re-reading an old diary or schoolbook. What can you take from your past into your future? Embrace the changing of the seasons and September's promise of renewal.

september 1–7 WEEK 1

DAY

DAY

DAY

DAY

DAY

NOTES

DAY

DAY

PRIORITIES

september 8-14 WEEK 2

DAY	

DAY	

DAY	

DAY	

DAY	

DAY	

DAY	

NOTES

PRIORITIES

september 15–21 WEEK 3

DAY

DAY

DAY

DAY

DAY

NOTES

DAY

DAY

PRIORITIES

september 22–28 WEEK 4

DAY

DAY

DAY

DAY

DAY

NOTES

DAY

DAY

PRIORITIES

september **29-30** WEEK 5

DAY

NOTES

DAY

PRIORITIES

OVERVIEW

Here are some questions to reflect on at the end of this month:

★ *How did September go for you?*

★ *Celebrate one thing you're proud of.*

★ *Acknowledge and let go of anything that went less well.*

★ *Set aside an afternoon to finish off any quick tasks or errands from this month, reset your space, and set your intentions and goals for the month ahead.*

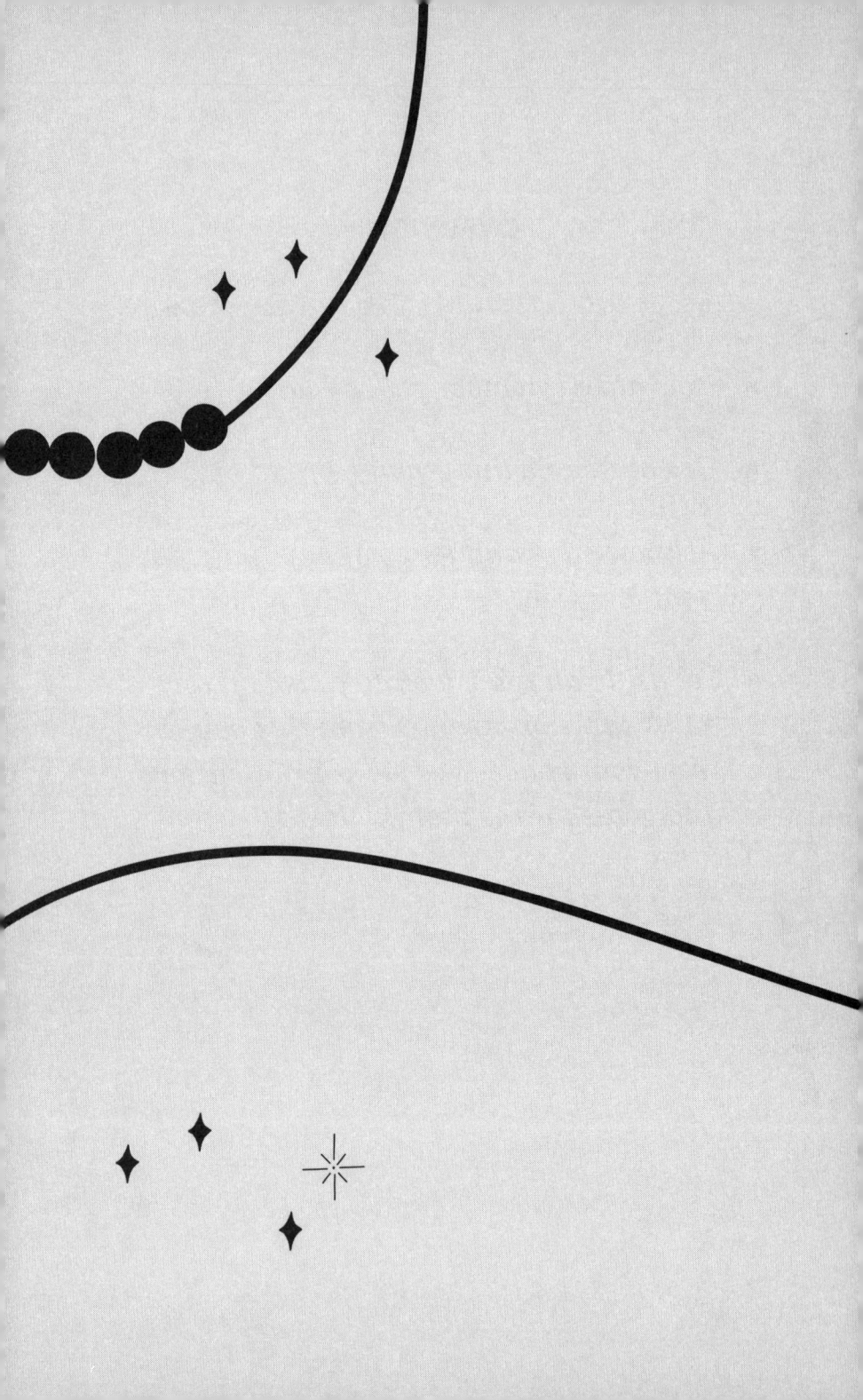

October

RED

Introduction

October is *Red*.

Nostalgic, reflective, bittersweet. As the leaves change and the air becomes crisp, *Red* is the ideal album to explore the complicated emotions that rise up in this season of change.

This month, use the lessons of *Red*—dealing with regret, extending compassion both to yourself and those who have hurt you, accepting complicated emotions that might both wound you and heal you—to accept yourself and your feelings more wholly.

As the year winds down, October is a time to become more introspective, looking back at the year you've had or even past years. The longing, emotional depth and intense detail of *Red*'s lyrics pull us immediately into Taylor's experience, so tangible you can see the stories she tells playing out over the warm russet tones of the album artwork.

It's such an immersive album that listening to it any time of year will take you back to the bright mornings and long cozy nights of autumn—maybe even, as many of Taylor's fans feel, to the autumn you first listened to the original release or to 2021's *Taylor's Version*. Of all her re-recordings, perhaps this one feels the most intimate and reflective, as Taylor noticeably revisits and lingers on her past feelings and this emotionally transformative chapter of her life.

You might use this October to look back on a similar season of your life, and make peace with it. Or, if you're in the midst of this kind of turbulence now, just be gentle with yourself.

This month, accept all your complicated feelings: be "happy, free, confused, and lonely at the same time." Find small moments of joy where you can, like the bright leaves on the trees before they fall. As Taylor does in *Red*, try to bring a curiosity and attentiveness to yourself, your life, and the world around you. Record those seemingly small details. Remember that where you are now will soon be a memory.

In the prologue to *Taylor's Version*, she writes "imagining your future might always take you on a detour back to the past." This October, look back to your past as well as accepting yourself as you are now—in all that messy, complicated glory.

Celebrate and commiserate with yourself, be curious about your feelings and observant of the world around you. Like October itself, *Red* is as cozy and mellow as it is aching with melancholy. Let this month be, like *Red*, a moment of precisely observed experiences, a blaze of autumn color.

Focus on curiosity, compassion, and introspection this month.

Try daily journaling without restricting or curating what you write.

Go back in time to a painful situation so that you can move past it.

Make a conscious decision to start afresh in whichever way you need it. Remember that loss and grief can help us to grow. Watch the autumn leaves, and realize that a new beginning can sometimes feel like an ending—or vice versa—it's all in the way you look at it.

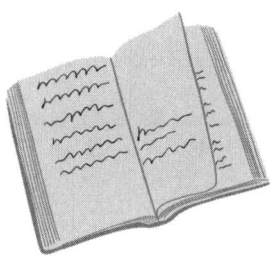

"*Like the colors in autumn, so bright,*

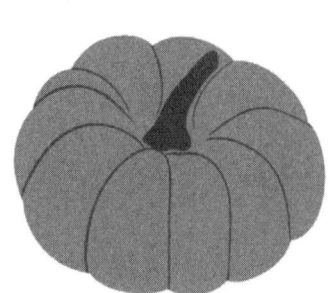

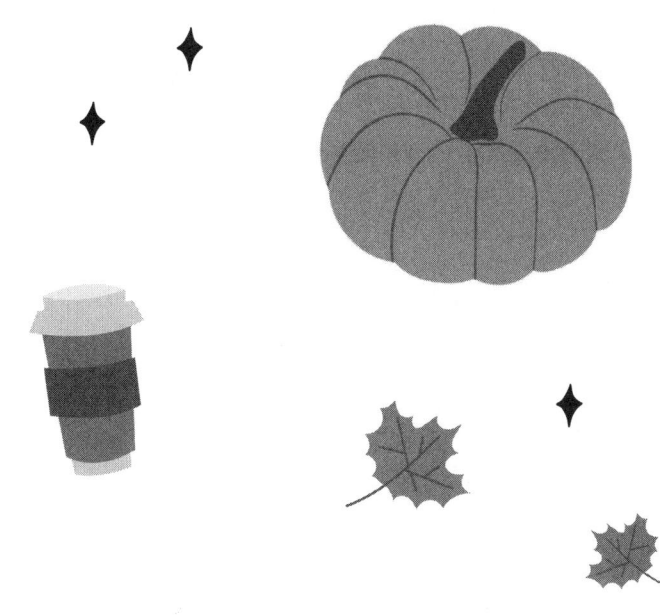

just before they lose it all"

"This is a state of grace"

This month, try a new routine of journaling at the start of each day. If you can, do this as soon as possible after waking up, and do it by hand.

Let it be messy and complicated—on scraps of paper, with cross outs, letting sentences trail off as new thoughts interrupt. Extend total grace to yourself and your feelings.

These diary entries might sometimes be a rant of self-pity that you would never express to anyone else, or a totally boring list of things you need to do that day, or a rehashing of something minor that keeps playing in your head. If you can't think of what to write, try and remember the day before in as much detail as possible.

It doesn't matter. The point is curiosity and compassion for yourself.

At the end of the month, read back all your diary entries and reflect on these questions:

What emotions kept recurring this month?
Name them as specifically as you can, e.g. disappointment, hope, nostalgia . . .

What details stand out for you from this month?
Is there something particularly evocative, such as a place you visited?

Are there any memories or past experiences that kept cropping up for you?

Why do you think you keep returning—is it to do with the time of year, interacting with a particular person, or a specific activity?

Is this a positive memory or a negative one? If it's negative, are you gaining something—perspective, closure, understanding—from returning to it?

Red

Red marked a turning point in Taylor's career, catching her at a
precise moment of flux. We can see her sudden maturity lyrically,
sonically, and even aesthetically. Gone are the fairy-tale gowns
and the heartbroken lamentations over first loves and the loss of
innocence; we're firmly in the disintegration of a serious, enduring
relationship and the confusion of its aftermath.

In both the album's title and the cover—Taylor with her head
down and face shadowed—we can see the inspiration from Joni
Mitchell's *Blue*, and the assertion that comes with this comparison:
this is Taylor as a mature, fully fledged singer-songwriter.

Red mixes styles of music, from country to rock and, for the first
time, pop music. This variety in genre stays cohesive and immersive
because of the specificity of detail in Taylor's songwriting. What
sets *Red*'s more upbeat songs like "I Knew You Were Trouble" apart
from her later pop music is the retention of diaristic storytelling,
making each song feel like a journal entry straight from Taylor's
head. "We Are Never Ever Getting Back Together," for example, is
light-hearted and tonally opposite from songs like "The Last Time."
Yet it recognizably takes place in the same world—a story of "indie
records" and long-distance phone calls, broken promises, and second
chances much regretted. And where "The Last Time" is pleading for
the subject to not waste this final chance—"This is the last time I'm
asking you this"—"We Are Never Getting Back Together" is clearly in
its frustrated aftermath.

While all Taylor's albums touch in some way on finding yourself and gaining independence, *Red* departs from *Fearless* and *Speak Now*'s sense of a young girl asserting her place in the world, standing on her own for the first time. Instead, Taylor is putting the pieces of herself back together again after merging them with someone else. As she sings about in "Nothing New," a "From the Vault" track featured on 2021's re-record, the gulf of time from eighteen to twenty-two can make you suddenly realize you "know nothing." "Nothing New" sees Taylor expand on and dive deeper into the negative effects of fame that she first explored in "The Lucky One"; these two songs as a set begin a strand of Taylor's songwriting that deals extensively with public image and the pressure that fame exerts on a person.

Perhaps more than any other re-recording so far, *Red*'s "From the Vault" tracks often see this expansion or deeper reflection on the themes of the original album. It's why *Taylor's Version* of *Red* has come to seem emblematic of the re-recording process. And it makes sense, for an album that in its first instance was already so preoccupied with revisiting the past. In all the Vault tracks, but, of course, especially with "All Too Well (Ten-Minute Version)," we see the power of an artist returning to their experiences with new skills and perspectives.

Taylor's choice to end her re-recording with a ten-minute song that had been cut down for the original release makes a satisfying conclusion to *Red*'s soul-searching lyrics and clear personal pain. Through returning to the pain and the bittersweet memories, Taylor found herself again, and then—almost a decade later—she returned with the power to now release the full version, inviting fans to immerse themselves in *Red*'s beautiful heartbroken world even more than before.

TEN-MINUTE ACTIVITIES

"I'd like to be my old self again, but I'm still trying to find it"

In *Red*'s original physical booklet, Taylor sums up the overarching theme with a line from Pablo Neruda's "Tonight I Can Write (the Saddest Lines)": "Love is so short, forgetting is so long." *Red* is the album of Taylor's with by far the most mentions of the word "remember." We're often told to stop ruminating on pain and the past, but sometimes the memories keep coming up until we turn to face them.

Take a blank piece of paper and a pen. Set a timer for ten minutes but otherwise try to remove all distractions. Now return to a painful experience or memory that you can't let go of. If it was a long-term situation, see if you can identify something precise.

Take yourself back there, and write it out. Don't stop, and see what details come up that you thought you'd forgotten.

In *Red*, it's clear that Taylor has lost something of herself in the turmoil of heartbreak. It's perhaps this which makes her obsession—through the whole album, but in "All Too Well" in particular—over memories and details so intensely haunting.

Through the detritus of change, loss, and heartbreak, we get a sense of Taylor sifting through the pieces for herself again. She recounts and reaffirms what happened and how she felt, clinging to the only things she now knows to be true.

With another piece of paper and another ten-minute timer, identify which parts of yourself you feel like you've lost.

What would make you feel like your old self again? Read back on what you've written, and see if there's an activity, place, or even a simple drink or meal that felt integral to you.

october 1–7 WEEK 1

DAY

DAY

DAY

DAY

DAY

NOTES

DAY

DAY

PRIORITIES

october 8-14 WEEK 2

DAY

DAY

DAY

DAY

DAY

NOTES

DAY

DAY

PRIORITIES

october 15–21 WEEK 3

DAY

DAY

DAY

DAY

DAY

NOTES

DAY

DAY

PRIORITIES

october 22–28 WEEK 4

DAY

DAY

DAY

DAY

DAY

NOTES

DAY

DAY

PRIORITIES

october **29–31** WEEK 5

DAY

DAY

DAY

NOTES

PRIORITIES

"ON A WEDNESDAY, IN A CAFÉ . . ."

Wading through complicated feelings and painful memories can leave you feeling heavy. Make sure you take some time this month for a fresh start. Remember that no emotion or situation lasts forever—and that sometimes, we need to actively jump into the new.

Find a Wednesday this month when you're free, and take yourself to a café. This time, leave the diary at home, and try to people-watch and observe as closely as possible, without returning to your own thoughts or ruminations.

Can you make this a purposeful moment to "Begin Again"?

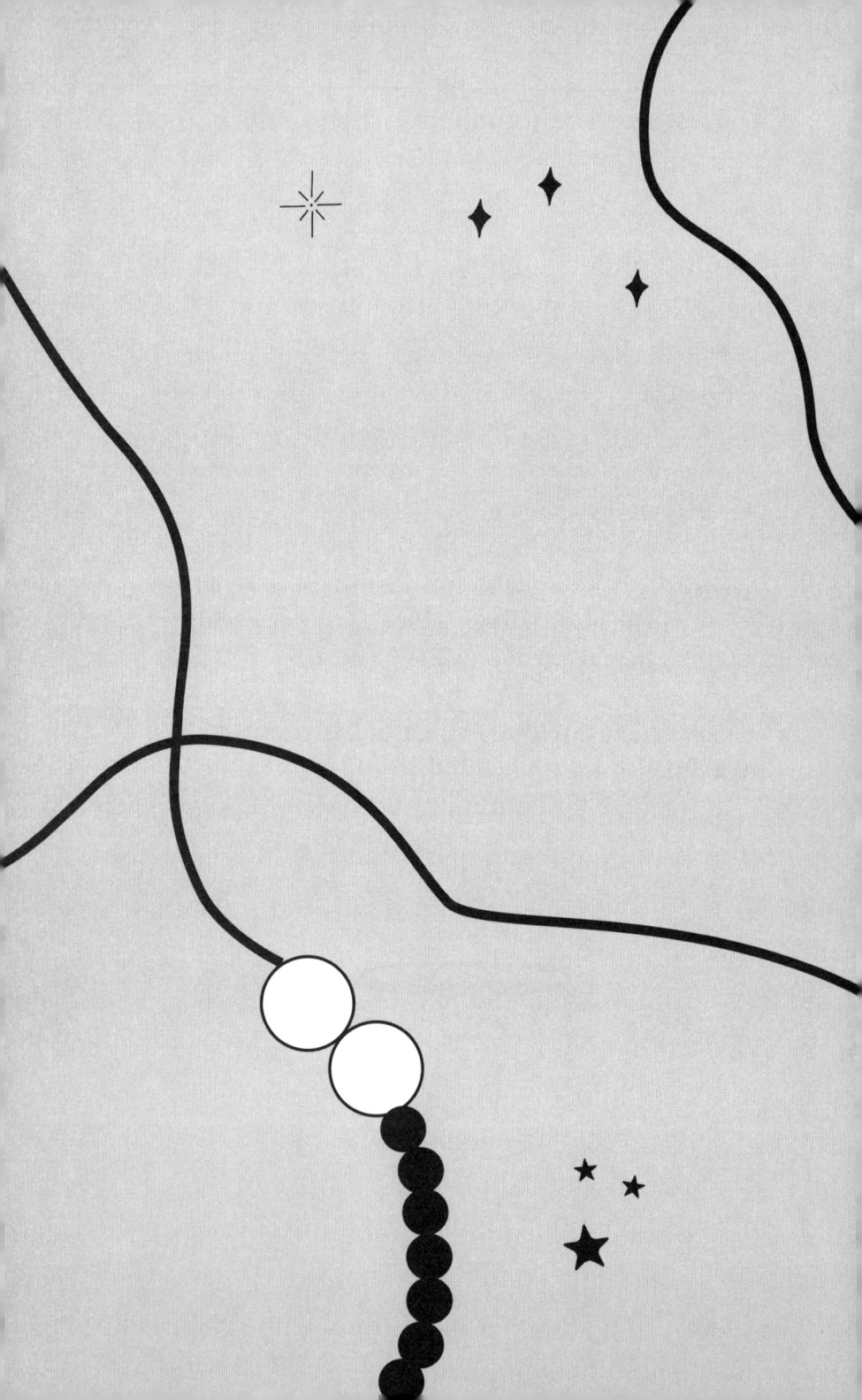

November

EVERMORE

Introduction

November is *evermore*.

We're back to the *folklore* forests of late summer, but the seasons have changed. It's "gray November," as Taylor sings in the haunting title track, "evermore."

November is a month for getting lost once more in storytelling and introspection. In this cold, often dreary month, take sustenance from the stories of others. Use the long nights to reflect on your own feelings and start to think about the end of the year.

After the transitional months of September and October, November no longer feels like a season of change or renewal. Instead, it seems to stretch on interminably. The days are cold and the nights are long; the leaves have fallen. But we can use this lull to look inward, or emulate animals all over the world and hibernate, taking a deliberate choice to do less and slow down.

With the seasonal holidays looming, before you know it there will be parties and festivities again, and then suddenly we're into a new year. Take the time while you can.

Like *folklore*, *evermore* was written in the middle of a global pandemic, and Taylor noted in the album's prologue that "this holiday season will be a lonely one for most of us." Whatever particular circumstances surround the holidays for you this year, take stock of how you feel about the season, and use some time this November to plan how you might be able to improve that experience.

Wrap up warm, and walk outside through the frosty landscapes.

Notice how life persists even through subdued colors and frozen ground.

November can be a time of year for heavy feelings. As Taylor does on *evermore*, take this heaviness and turn it around in your hand, reflecting inward, going deeper into emotions with character studies and storytelling.

Embrace the cold and bleakness, and see what the stark landscape reveals back to you.

November is the perfect month to hunker down and reflect.

In this quiet month, turn to reading and writing, a tradition in many parts of the world as the days get shorter and darker.

Write letters to those you miss, even if you don't send them.

Find comfort in the stories of others, and see how you can use them to reflect on your own journey.

Embrace and accept where you are, but also start to plan for the end of the year, and the next year to come. What habits do you want to take forward with you? How can you make the holiday season enjoyable?

Look for moments of peace and clarity, like the sun coming out unexpectedly on a November morning.

"November flush

and your flannel cure"

LETTER WRITING

Take inspiration from Taylor's direct-address mode of songwriting on *evermore* by writing letters to important people in your life, or even those who are no longer in your life.

This could be your "dorothea," or it could be the person Dorothea seems to address in "'tis the damn season." It could be your "marjorie," calling back to the lessons and wisdom learned from a loved one who has now passed away, or any of the other characters in *evermore*'s songs.

Pay attention to how it feels putting your vulnerabilities on paper. When you're writing to someone you don't speak to anymore, or perhaps someone you communicate with mainly in back-and-forth conversations, it can feel exposing to write about your thoughts and feelings in detail, without knowing how they'll respond.

Could you send this letter? What do you think their response would be?

If you choose not to, what would you most like to say to this person? What have you learned from having them in your life?

"Yes, I'm doing better"

Now take inspiration from "closure," and write a letter only for yourself.

Use this to give yourself closure or let go of something negative. Whether it's an imagined response to a situation that still causes you pain, or a triumphant acknowledgment of moving on, lean into whatever makes you feel at peace and gives you a sense of resolution.

As Taylor sings, don't use closure as an excuse to smooth out or forget unpleasant feelings. We can close a chapter while still acknowledging the impact it has had on us.

Letting go doesn't mean that it no longer matters.

evermore

From glancing at the album covers to listening side by side, it's clear that *evermore* is a sister album to *folklore*—the albums' songs were written in the same period, with similar aesthetics, characters, and landscapes, and have many of the same co-writers and producers. Like *folklore*, *evermore* blends folk, indie, and alternative pop, combining introspection with intricately detailed portraits of fictional characters. Taylor utilizes the same techniques with vividly imagined names, locations, and personal histories for her characters. But on one of the more abstract—and, indeed, markedly more positive—tracks, "gold rush," she seems to nod to listeners with a subtle clue.

"My mind turns your life into folklore," she sings on this dreamy, heady ode to an idealized lover. There's a blurring of the personal and the imagined on *evermore*, almost as if, in going deeper into the worlds she created on the former album, Taylor is beginning to recognize the ways her mind might have transformed her own experiences into fiction. With her song "marjorie," Taylor takes this trick of naming and grounding her fictional characters and applies it to real life, with an ode to her late grandmother. *evermore* has another layer of introspection compared to *folklore*, and a sense of maturity evident in the characters that move from high school sweethearts to disillusioned wives and complicated adult women with their own pasts.

Despite its diffuse subjects and settings, there's a thematic cohesiveness to *evermore*: a sense of a journey, out of despair and hopelessness, toward release and acceptance, encapsulated most fully on songs like "evermore" and "closure." When positioning the tracks along this journey, the songs most filled with pain are often most concretely fictional, such as the obsessive refrain of "right where you left me," where the speaker remains frozen at the restaurant where her heart was broken.

In the song "coney island," a desolate amusement park and introspective speaker lead to an expansive bridge that seems to hint at experiences throughout Taylor's life, picked out by nods to the unhappy "birthday" of *Red*'s "The Moment I Knew" and the "bluest skies" in "Dear John" from *Speak Now*. Sitting within the imagery of desolate rides and twinkling lights, we're left with a profound sense of Taylor's ability as a songwriter and storyteller: crafting stories from past pain and present uncertainties, propelling herself onward on a journey towards growth and hope.

Reclaiming Stories

"Now I'm begging for footnotes in the story of your life"

When something or someone makes us feel overlooked, misunderstood, or unappreciated, we can feel like we lose autonomy over our own choices.

If you feel like that over this month, try using fictional stories to reclaim your own narrative, moving from a story that is not yours to taking ownership.

At the Toronto International Film Festival in 2022, Taylor revealed *Sense and Sensibility* was a story she returned to repeatedly while writing *evermore*.

What stories can help you process this time in your life?

You might want to turn to something that relates to what you're going through—whether that's a coming-of-age story, a romance, or a family drama—but if that doesn't appeal, try reading something completely different. As Taylor did, turn to a classic and see what lessons and experiences are common to everyone over time.

What story or fictional character makes you feel the most seen?

"'tis the damn season"

Toward the end of November, start thinking about next month.

Is there anything that you often find difficult during the holidays?

It might be the lack of downtime, the extra socialization, or the focus on "cheer" and consumerism—whatever it is, acknowledging it early can help you prepare to deal with it.

Make a plan to address this in whatever way you can—it could be as simple as blocking out a few days in December to focus on yourself and what you want.

Gearing up to the holidays can also be a powerfully nostalgic and resonant time. As Taylor sings, around this time of year "time flies, messy as the mud on your truck tires."

When you think of the holiday season, where are you brought back to? Is there a strong positive or negative memory?
  Or is there a behavior you find yourself slipping back into, even as you've outgrown it? What situations prompt this, and can you avoid them?

"You haven't met the new me yet"

"happiness" captures a fleeting but powerful moment of change, recognizable to anyone who has gone through an upheaval in their personal life. You know the "old you" isn't able to cope with these challenges, but the "new you" isn't here yet.

In fact, they're being formed through the very pain you're growing through.

The beauty of "happiness" lies in the core of self-belief and hope in a very despairing song. Can you take lessons from this, and think of a habit or ritual for "the new you"?

What's something you could do each day that would make you feel like the new you?

Small steps are the only way out of difficult situations.

november 1–7 WEEK 1

DAY

DAY

DAY

DAY

DAY

NOTES

DAY

DAY

PRIORITIES

november 8–14 WEEK 2

DAY

DAY

DAY

DAY

DAY

NOTES

DAY

DAY

PRIORITIES

november 15–21 WEEK 3

DAY

DAY

DAY

DAY

DAY

NOTES

DAY

DAY

PRIORITIES

DAY

DAY

DAY

DAY

DAY

NOTES

DAY

DAY

PRIORITIES

november **29–30** WEEK 5

DAY	

NOTES

DAY	

PRIORITIES

OVERVIEW

Here are some questions to reflect on at the end of this month:

★ *How did November go for you?*

★ *Celebrate one thing you're proud of.*

★ *Acknowledge and let go of anything that went less well.*

★ *Set aside an afternoon to finish off any quick tasks or errands from this month, reset your space, and set your intentions and goals for the month ahead.*

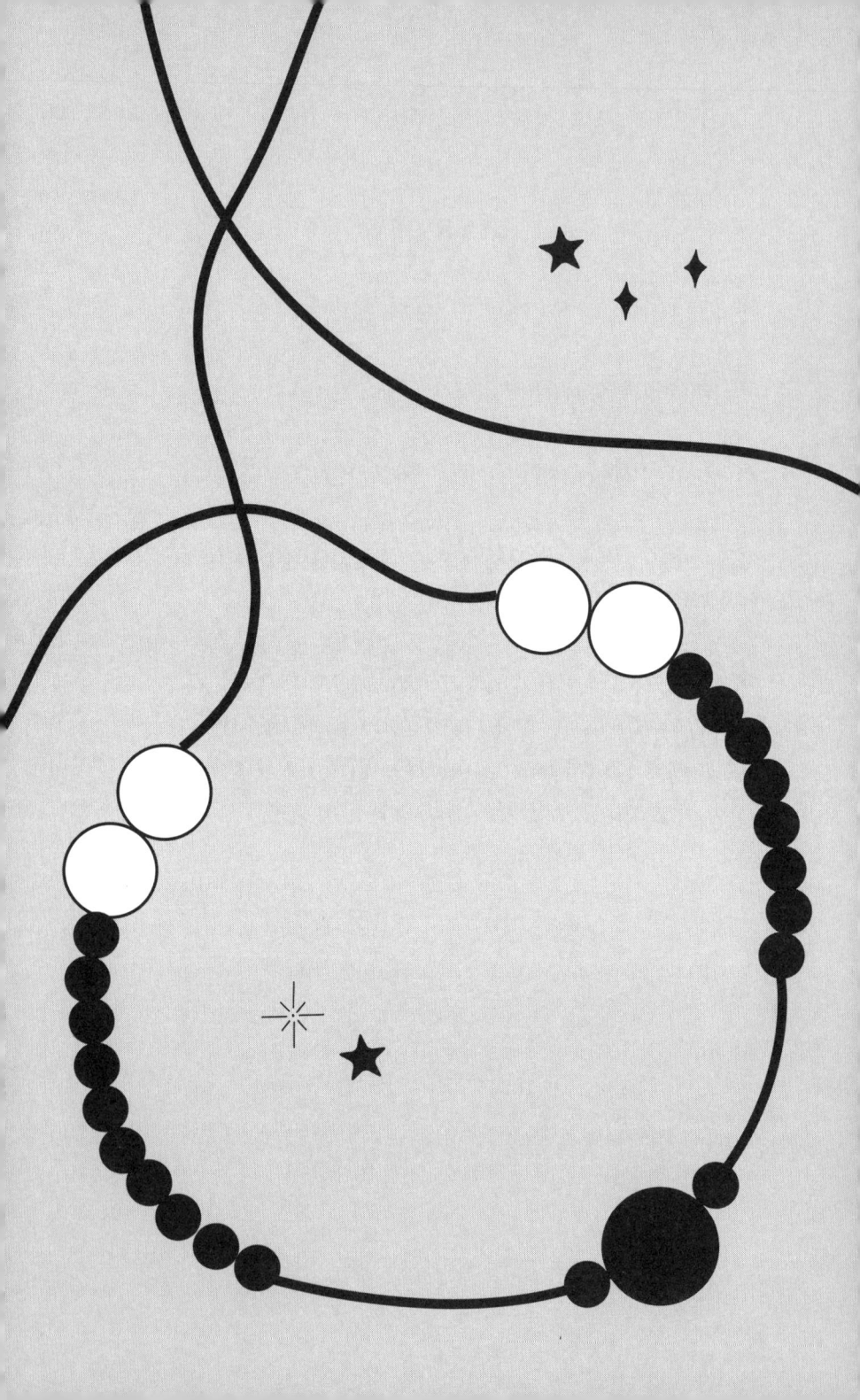

December

MIDNIGHTS

Introduction

December is *Midnights*.

December brings us to *Midnights*, which in Taylor's own words is all about "the stories of 13 sleepless nights scattered throughout my life." It's about looking back and closing chapters. With its metaphors of clocks winding down, it has a feeling of reckoning—with yourself, with your life—within a kind of waiting room, a countdown for the next chapter of your story.

During the longest nights of the year, and the days between Christmas and New Year—a sometimes confusing mixture of festivity and quiet clarity—*Midnights* has a song for the dizzying range of emotions, whether acoustic and contemplative, or bold and sparkling.

This December, let go of anything that may not have gone to plan this year. Accept the sleepless nights of a closing chapter and remember to celebrate your highs as well as analyzing your lows.

Midnights encapsulates the full spectrum of a year with its themes of reflection, late-night thoughts, and unresolved emotions. The synth-pop and ethereal melodies have the feeling of a soft, slow winter's night, evoked in dreamy, shimmering tracks like "Snow on the Beach," where Taylor and Lana Del Rey's echoing evocations of "aurora borealis green" sum up a starry winter's evening. Tracks like "Bejeweled," meanwhile, quite literally "shimmer" with all the promise of a Christmas or New Year's party.

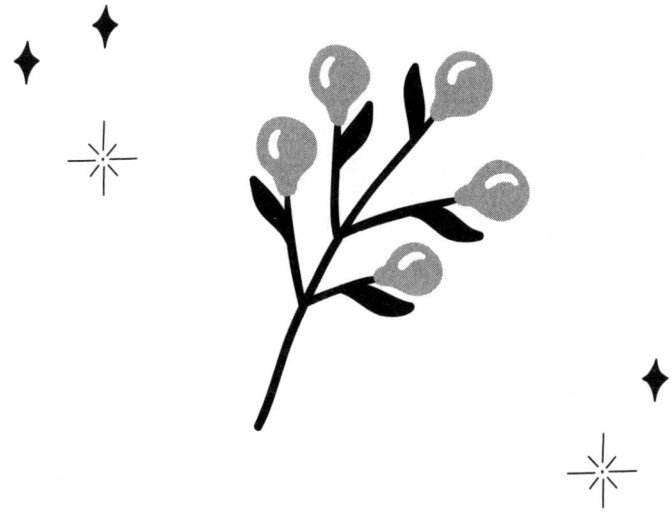

December is always a month of transition, where we begin to close chapters and prepare for new beginnings. Use *Midnights* as inspiration for this season of your life: explore the ways you've changed and the ways you're still changing, the mistakes you regret, and the moments you're most proud of.

On New Year's Eve, in the last gasp of the month and the year, drink in the cold air and hope, as Taylor writes in *Midnights'* prologue, "That just maybe, when the clock strikes twelve . . . we'll meet ourselves."

This December, let go of your regrets and mistakes. Sometimes we have to return to these low moments to gain space and perspective in order to appreciate our successes. Return to your goals set in January, and be proud of how far you've come.

Smear on the glittering eyeshadow of Taylor on the *Midnights* album cover and go out to celebrate the end of the year. Allow brightness and festivity to crowd into the dark days.

But find moments of peace too. Be present in all the "sweet nothings"—simple time with loved ones, or solo walks looking at the bright lights.

Prepare for next year with the confidence that you have grown and are still growing. This New Year's Eve, feel confident that next year will be as bright and as dark as this one—as full of hope and pain—and remember that all your midnights have made you who you are.

"'Cause there were pages turned

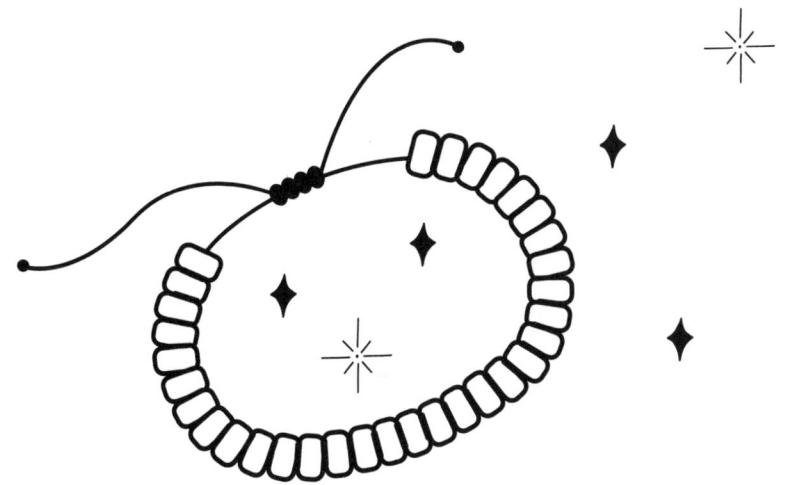

with the bridges burned"

YEARLY REFLECTIONS

How did this year go for you?

Try to focus less on the goals you might have set, and more on how you felt: Was it a year of happiness? Or if not happiness, did you manage to find peace?

As well as the good, return to the moment where you felt most alone this year. As Taylor sings about in "You're On Your Own, Kid," sometimes it takes reaching what feels like the top to realize how isolated you feel.

But maybe you can't have one without the other. Maybe you would never have had your best moment this year without experiencing your worst. Or maybe the best moment is still to come—you'll know when you get there.

Either way, be proud that you're the only person who is going to get you where you need to be. Reflect on your year, and get ready to turn the page to a new one.

Midnights

Blending the synth pop of *1989* with the introspective storytelling of *folklore* and *evermore*, *Midnights* is the dark, moody, restless return of a newly mature Taylor to her pop prime.

Lyrically, she pushes further into her own flaws and self-analysis with songs like "Anti-Hero" and "Midnight Rain." More clearly and succinctly than before, she weaves together two key strands of her storytelling: romantic growth and disappointments, and the pressures of fame and public image. In "Anti-Hero," she could be speaking to her fans or about her personal relationships with the knowing nod: "It must be exhausting always rooting for the anti-hero," followed by a more direct fear of being abandoned that wakes her in the middle of the night. "Midnight Rain" braids the two fears closer together with wistful lyrics about the conflict between love and ambition, and the bittersweet decisions Taylor makes in order to achieve her goals. "All of me changed like midnight," she sings, her voice soft and haunting beneath loud backing vocals warped to the point of androgyny. That's another key theme of *Midnights*— the distortion of sounds and vocals mimicking Taylor's refusal to conform and do what's expected.

This is not quite the hyper-specific clue-dropping of her earlier albums—timelines are obscured by the central theme of midnights throughout her life—although there's fun to be had with scouring both the lyrics and the vastly differing musical styles for hints about which "midnight" she's looking back on.

Midnights really comes into its own on the songs that examine

Taylor's life and ambitions. Whether it's the high-school-prom narrative of fan favorite "You're On Your Own, Kid" or the wry admissions of manipulation in "Mastermind" and "Dear Reader," this is an album that—despite all the mess and regret and dark emotions bubbling under the surface—is poised and confident. The heartbreak and conflict, unusually for Taylor, is filtered through time and shifting perspectives.

We come away with the sense that Taylor's decision to look back into the past for these songs is only galvanizing her for her next steps, storing up reminders of who she is and where's she been—and, most importantly, perhaps, the fact that she always comes out on top. The fact that *Midnights* was then followed by the unpoised, supercharged turbulence of *The Tortured Poets Department* only goes to show that Taylor is always one step ahead.

Celebrate Your Successes

"Karma" is one of the most jubilant songs on *Midnights*, reflecting how confidence in yourself and your integrity is the best reward. There's a reason Taylor chose it to close out the Eras Tour—perhaps the ultimate proof of her success—in a storm of fireworks and multicolored outfits.

But what "Karma" really celebrates is not the big wins, but the small ones—the ways you make yourself proud when no one is looking. There's nothing better than enjoying little moments of peace because you know you deserve them.

Look back on your year, and celebrate unconventional successes. These could be:

A moment you could have responded to unpleasantly, but didn't.
A kind act you did when you didn't have to.
A moment of faith when you had no proof things would all work out.

Whatever keeps your "side of the street clean" is worth celebrating!

"*Get it off my desk*"

This time of year can be overwhelming, swinging as it does from quiet nights alone to excesses of socializing and busyness. It's made even more intense by the new year hanging over us—we can be gripped by a sense of time running out if we're not careful to frame it the right way.

Try to free yourself from a panicky sense of things-not-done, and try not to get bogged down already by what you have to achieve next year.

Get a piece of paper—that you'll throw away later—and clear your mind by getting it all out: everything you wanted to do but didn't, everything you tried to do but failed, everything you'd love to do next year but already feel overwhelmed by.

Then rip it up.

And use the next page to set only one goal, with purpose and clarity, for the next year:

"IF YOU FAIL TO PLAN, YOU PLAN TO FAIL"

Inspired by "Mastermind," set your New Year's resolution—while acknowledging, as Taylor wryly does in the song, that we are never as in control of our scheming as we might think.

Cut through the noise of this time of year—maybe all the achievements of the people you're catching up with, the all-or-nothing narratives of Christmas films, or the start of "new year new me" online buzz—and set just one goal, focused only on self-growth rather than achieving something external.

MY NEW YEAR'S RESOLUTION:

....

....

....

....

december 1–7 WEEK 1

DAY

DAY

DAY

DAY

DAY

NOTES

DAY

PRIORITIES

DAY

december 8-14 WEEK 2

DAY

DAY

DAY

DAY

DAY

NOTES

DAY

DAY

PRIORITIES

december 15–21 WEEK 3

DAY

DAY

DAY

DAY

DAY

NOTES

DAY

DAY

PRIORITIES

DAY

DAY

DAY

DAY

DAY

NOTES

DAY

DAY

PRIORITIES

december **29–31** WEEK 5

DAY

DAY

DAY

NOTES

PRIORITIES

OVERVIEW

Here are some questions to reflect on at the end of this month:

★ *How did December go for you?*

★ *Celebrate one thing you're proud of.*

★ *Acknowledge and let go of anything that went less well.*

★ *Set aside an afternoon to finish off any quick tasks or errands from this month, reset your space, and set your intentions and goals for the month ahead.*

Quoted Material

SONG LYRICS

January: *reputation*

p.5: "Dancing with Our Hands Tied" by Taylor Swift (Big Machine). Lyrics by Max Martin / Oscar Holter / Shellback / Taylor Swift © 2017 (Kobalt Music Publishing Ltd. / Universal Music Publishing Group / Warner Chappell Music, Inc.).

p.8: "... Ready for It?" by Taylor Swift (Big Machine). Lyrics by Ali Payami / Shellback / Max Martin / Taylor Swift © 2017 (Universal Music Publishing Group / Kobalt Music Publishing Ltd / Warner Chappell Music, Inc. / Sony/ATV Music Publishing, LLC).

p.12: "Delicate" by Taylor Swift (Big Machine). Lyrics by Taylor Swift / Max Martin / Shellback © 2017 (Universal Music Publishing Group / Kobalt Music Publishing Ltd.).

p.14: "New Year's Day" by Taylor Swift (Big Machine). Lyrics by Taylor Swift / Jack Antonoff © 2017 (Universal Music Publishing Group / Sony/ATV Music Publishing, LLC).

p.16: "So It Goes..." by Taylor Swift (Big Machine). Lyrics by Taylor Swift / Oscar Görres / Max Martin / Shellback © 2017 (Universal Music Publishing Group / Kobalt Music Publishing Ltd / Warner Chappell Music, Inc.).

p.23: "Call It What You Want" by Taylor Swift (Big Machine). Lyrics by Taylor Swift / Jack Antonoff © 2017 (Universal Music Publishing Group / Sony/ATV Music Publishing, LLC).

p.23: "King of My Heart" by Taylor Swift (Big Machine). Lyrics by Taylor Swift / Max Martin / Shellback © 2017 (Universal Music Publishing Group / Kobalt Music Publishing Ltd.).

February: *The Tortured Poets Department*

p.26: "So Long, London" by Taylor Swift (Republic). Lyrics by Taylor Swift / Aaron Dessner © 2024 (Universal Music Publishing Group / Sony/ATV Music Publishing, LLC).

p.30: "Fortnight" by Taylor Swift and Post Malone (Republic). Lyrics by Taylor Swift / Post Malone / Jack Antonoff © 2024 (Universal Music Publishing Group).

p.32: "I Can Do It with a Broken Heart" by Taylor Swift (Republic). Lyrics by Taylor Swift / Jack Antonoff © 2024 (Universal Music Publishing Group).

p.34: "loml" by Taylor Swift (Republic). Lyrics by Taylor Swift / Aaron Dessner © 2024 (Universal Music Publishing Group / Sony/ATV Music Publishing, LLC).

p.34: "Who's Afraid of Little Old Me?" by Taylor Swift (Republic). Lyrics by Taylor Swift © 2024 (Universal Music Publishing Group).

p.35: "Clara Bow" by Taylor Swift (Republic). Lyrics by Taylor Swift / Aaron Dessner © 2024 (Universal Music Publishing Group / Sony/ATV Music Publishing, LLC).

p.35: "The Tortured Poets Department" by Taylor Swift (Republic). Lyrics by Taylor Swift / Jack Antonoff © 2024 (Universal Music Publishing Group).

p.36: "The Alchemy" by Taylor Swift (Republic). Lyrics by Taylor Swift / Jack Antonoff © 2024 (Universal Music Publishing Group).

p.38: "Down Bad" by Taylor Swift (Republic). Lyrics by Taylor Swift / Jack Antonoff © 2024 (Universal Music Publishing Group).

March: *Speak Now*

All songs by Taylor Swift (Big Machine (2010) / Republic (2023)). All lyrics by Taylor Swift © 2010 (Universal Music Publishing Group).

p.52: "Enchanted"
p.57: "Long Live"
p.58: "Sparks Fly"
p.59: "Last Kiss"
p.59: "Back to December"
p.60: "Dear John"
p.61: "Innocent"

April: *Fearless*

p.71: "Change" by Taylor Swift (Big Machine (2008) / Republic (2021)). Lyrics by Taylor Swift © 2008 (Universal Music Publishing Group).

p.71: "Fearless" by Taylor Swift (Big Machine (2008) / Republic (2021)). Lyrics by Taylor Swift / Liz Rose / Hillary Lindsey © 2008 (Universal Music Publishing Group / BMG Rights Management / Sony/ ATV Music Publishing, LLC / Anthem Entertainment).

p.74: "You Belong with Me" by Taylor Swift (Big Machine (2008) / Republic (2021)). Lyrics by Taylor Swift / Liz Rose © 2008 (Universal Music Publishing Group / Orbison Music, LLC. / Warner Chappell Music, Inc.).

p.79: "Love Story" by Taylor Swift (Big Machine (2008) / Republic (2021)). Lyrics by Taylor Swift © 2008 (Universal Music Publishing Group).

p.82: "The Way I Loved You" by Taylor Swift (Big Machine (2008) / Republic (2021)). Lyrics by Taylor Swift / John Rich © 2008 (Universal Music Publishing Group / Kobalt Music Publishing Ltd.).

p.89: "White Horse" by Taylor Swift (Big Machine (2008) / Republic (2021)). Lyrics by Taylor Swift / Liz Rose © 2008 (Universal Music Publishing Group / Sony/ ATV Music Publishing, LLC / Anthem Entertainment).

May: *Taylor Swift*

p.96: "Our Song" by Taylor Swift (Big Machine). Lyrics by Taylor Swift © 2006 (Universal Music Publishing Group).

p.101: "The Outside" by Taylor Swift (Big Machine). Lyrics by Taylor Swift © 2006 (Universal Music Publishing Group).

p.101: "Cold as You" by Taylor Swift (Big Machine). Lyrics by Taylor Swift / Liz Rose © 2006 (Universal Music Publishing Group / Sony/ATV Music Publishing, LLC / Anthem Entertainment).

p.102: "Picture to Burn" by Taylor Swift (Big Machine). Lyrics by Taylor Swift / Liz Rose © 2006 (Universal Music Publishing Group / Sony/ATV Music Publishing, LLC / Anthem Entertainment).

p.103: "A Place in This World" by Taylor Swift (Big Machine). Lyrics by Taylor Swift / Angelo Petraglia / Robert Ellis Orrall © 2006 (Universal Music Publishing Group / Orrall Fixation Music / Songtrust Ave / Kobalt Music Publishing Ltd.).

June: *Lover*

p.118: "Cruel Summer" by Taylor Swift (Republic). Lyrics by Taylor Swift / Jack Antonoff / Annie Clark © 2019 (Universal Music Publishing Group / Sony/ATV Music Publishing, LLC / Hipgnosis Songs Group).

p.122: "Afterglow" by Taylor Swift (Republic). Lyrics by Taylor Swift / Adam King Feeney / Louis Bell / Matthew Tavares © 2019 (Universal Music Publishing Group / Sony/ATV Music Publishing, LLC / Third Side Music, Inc. / Quiet as Kept Music, Inc.).

p.122: "Cornelia Street" by Taylor Swift (Republic). Lyrics by Taylor Swift © 2019 (Universal Music Publishing Group).

p.126: "The Archer" by Taylor Swift (Republic). Lyrics by Taylor Swift / Jack Antonoff © 2019 (Universal Music Publishing Group / Sony/ATV Music Publishing, LLC).

p.126: "Death by a Thousand Cuts" by Taylor Swift (Republic). Lyrics by Taylor Swift / Jack Antonoff © 2019 (Universal Music Publishing Group / Sony/ATV Music Publishing, LLC).

p.127: "Lover" by Taylor Swift (Republic). Lyrics by Taylor Swift © 2019 (Universal Music Publishing Group).

p.128: "Daylight" by Taylor Swift (Republic). Lyrics by Taylor Swift © 2019 (Universal Music Publishing Group).

July: *1989*

p.142: "New Romantics" by Taylor Swift (Big Machine (2014) / Republic (2023)). Lyrics by Taylor Swift / Max Martin / Shellback © 2014 (Universal Music Publishing Group / Kobalt Music Publishing Ltd.).

p.146: "Welcome to New York" by Taylor Swift (Big Machine (2014) / Republic (2023)). Lyrics by Taylor Swift / Ryan Tedder © 2014 (Universal Music Publishing Group / Concord Music Publishing LLC).

p.146: "Mean" by Taylor Swift (Big Machine (2010) / Republic (2023)). Lyrics by Taylor Swift © 2010 (Universal Music Publishing Group).

p.147: "You Are in Love" by Taylor Swift (Big Machine (2014) / Republic (2023)).

Lyrics by Taylor Swift / Jack Antonoff © 2014 (Universal Music Publishing Group / Sony/ATV Music Publishing, LLC).

p.147: "Slut" by Taylor Swift (Republic). Lyrics by Taylor Swift / Patrik Berger / Jack Antonoff © 2023 (Universal Music Publishing Group, Sony/ATV Music Publishing LLC, Kobalt Music Publishing Ltd.).

p.155: "Out of the Woods" by Taylor Swift (Big Machine (2014) / Republic (2023)). Lyrics by Taylor Swift / Jack Antonoff © 2014 (Universal Music Publishing Group / Sony/ATV Music Publishing, LLC).

p.155: "Is It Over Now?" by Taylor Swift (Republic). Lyrics by Taylor Swift / Jack Antonoff © 2023 (Universal Music Publishing Group / Sony/ATV Music Publishing, LLC).

August: *folklore*

All songs by Taylor Swift (Republic). All lyrics by Taylor Swift / Aaron Dessner © 2020 (Universal Music Publishing Group / Sony/ATV Music Publishing, LLC) unless stated otherwise.

p:162: "august" by Taylor Swift (Republic). Lyrics by Taylor Swift / Jack Antonoff © 2020 (Universal Music Publishing Group / Sony/ATV Music Publishing, LLC).

p.164: "the 1"

p.165: "mirrorball" by Taylor Swift (Republic). Lyrics by Taylor Swift / Jack Antonoff © 2020 (Universal Music Publishing Group / Sony/ATV Music Publishing, LLC).

p.167: "my tears ricochet" by Taylor Swift (Republic). Lyrics by Taylor Swift © 2020 (Universal Music Publishing Group).

p.168: "cardigan"

p.168: "betty" by Taylor Swift (Republic). Lyrics by Taylor Swift / William Bowery © 2020 (Universal Music Publishing Group).

p.169: "peace"

p.169: "the lakes" by Taylor Swift (Republic). Lyrics by Taylor Swift /

Jack Antonoff © 2020 (Universal Music Publishing Group / Sony/ATV Music Publishing, LLC).

p.171: "seven"

September: *The Tortured Poets Department: The Anthology*

All songs by Taylor Swift (Republic). All lyrics by Taylor Swift / Aaron Dessner © 2024 (Universal Music Publishing Group / Sony/ATV Music Publishing, LLC) unless stated otherwise.

p.184: "The Black Dog." Lyrics by Taylor Swift © 2024 (Universal Music Publishing Group).

p.188: "I Hate It Here"

p.189: "Chloe or Sam or Sophia or Marcus"

p.189: "How Did It End?"

p.190: "The Albatross"

p.190: "Cassandra"

p.191: "The Prophecy"

p.192: "thanK you aIMee"

p.192: "Peter." Lyrics by Taylor Swift © 2024 (Universal Music Publishing Group).

p.193: "So High School"

October: *Red*

p.202: "22" by Taylor Swift (Big Machine (2012) / Republic (2021)). Lyrics by Taylor Swift / Max Martin / Shellback © 2012 (Universal Music Publishing Group / Kobalt Music Publishing Ltd.).

p.206: "Red" by Taylor Swift (Big Machine (2012) / Republic (2021)). Lyrics by Taylor Swift © 2012 (Universal Music Publishing Group).

p.208: "State of Grace" by Taylor Swift (Big Machine (2012) / Republic (2021)). Lyrics by Taylor Swift © 2012 (Universal Music Publishing Group).

p.210: "We Are Never Ever Getting Back Together" by Taylor Swift (Big Machine (2012) / Republic (2021)). Lyrics by Taylor Swift / Max Martin / Shellback © 2012 (Universal Music Publishing Group / Kobalt Music Publishing Ltd.).

p.210: "The Last Time" by Taylor Swift and Gary Lightbody (Big Machine (2012) / Republic (2021)). Lyrics by Taylor Swift / Gary Lightbody / Garret Lee © 2012 (Universal Music Publishing Group / Concord Music Publishing LLC).

p.211: "Nothing New" by Taylor Swift and Phoebe Bridgers (Republic). Lyrics by Taylor Swift © 2021 (Universal Music Publishing Group).

p.212: "All Too Well" by Taylor Swift (Big Machine (2012) / Republic (2021)). Lyrics by Taylor Swift / Liz Rose © 2012 (Universal Music Publishing Group / Warner Chappell Music, Inc.).

p.219: "Begin Again" by Taylor Swift (Big Machine (2012) / Republic (2021)). Lyrics by Taylor Swift © 2012 (Universal Music Publishing Group).

November: *evermore*

All songs by Taylor Swift (Republic). All lyrics by Taylor Swift / Aaron Dessner © 2020 (Universal Music Publishing Group / Sony/ATV Music Publishing, LLC) unless stated otherwise.

p.222: "evermore" by Taylor Swift and Bon Iver (Republic). Lyrics by Taylor Swift / Justin Vernon / William Bowery © 2020 (Universal Music Publishing Group / Kobalt Music Publishing Ltd.).

p.226: "champagne problems" by Taylor Swift (Republic). Lyrics by Taylor Swift / William Bowery © 2020 (Universal Music Publishing Group).

p.229: "closure"

p.230: "gold rush" by Taylor Swift (Republic). Lyrics by Taylor Swift / Jack Antonoff © 2020 (Universal Music Publishing Group / Sony/ATV Music Publishing, LLC).

p.232: "tolerate it"

p.233: "'tis the damn season"

p.234: "happiness"

December: *Midnights*

All songs by Taylor Swift (Republic). All lyrics by Taylor Swift / Jack Antonoff © 2022 (Universal Music Publishing Group / Sony/ATV Music Publishing, LLC) unless stated otherwise.

p.244: "Snow on the Beach" by Taylor Swift and Lana Del Rey (Republic). Lyrics by Taylor Swift / Lana Del Rey / Jack Antonoff © 2022 (Universal Music Publishing Group / Sony/ATV Music Publishing, LLC).

p.244: "Bejeweled"

p.248: "You're on Your Own, Kid"

p.251: "Anti-Hero"

p.251: "Midnight Rain"

p.253: "Karma" by Taylor Swift (Republic). Lyrics by Taylor Swift / Jack Antonoff / Jahaan Sweet / Keanu Beats / Sounwave © 2022 (Universal Music Publishing Group, Sony/ATV Music Publishing LLC, Kobalt Music Publishing Ltd.).

p.254: "Lavender Haze" by Taylor Swift (Republic). Lyrics by Taylor Swift / Jack Antonoff / Jahaan Sweet / Sounwave / Sam Dew / Zoe Kravitz © 2022 (Universal Music Publishing Group, Sony/ATV Music Publishing LLC, Kobalt Music Publishing Ltd.).

p.255: "Mastermind"

TEXT QUOTES

p.5: Taylor Swift, "Prologue." *reputation* album (Big Machine, 2017).

p.34: Taylor Swift, "Epilogue." *The Tortured Poets Department* album (Republic, 2024).

p.48: Taylor Swift, "Prologue." *Speak Now (Taylor's Version)* album (Republic, 2023).

p.56: Taylor Swift, "Liner notes." *Speak Now* album (Big Machine, 2010).

p.70: Taylor Swift, "Liner notes." *Fearless* album (Big Machine, 2008).

p.78: Taylor Swift, "Prologue." *Fearless (Taylor's Version)* album (Republic, 2021).

p.92: Taylor Swift. Quoted in John Preston, "Taylor Swift: the 19-year-old country music star conquering America—and now Britain." *Daily Telegraph*, April 29, 2009.

p.147: Taylor Swift, "Prologue." *1989 (Taylor's Version)* album (Republic, 2023).

p.203: Taylor Swift, "Liner notes." *Red (Taylor's Version)* album (Republic, 2021).

p.212: Pablo Neruda, "Tonight I Can Write (the Saddest Lines)." Quoted in Taylor Swift, "Liner notes." *Red* (Big Machine, 2012).

p.222: Taylor Swift, "Prologue." *evermore* album (Republic, 2020).

p.245: Taylor Swift, "Prologue." *Midnights* album (Republic, 2022).

$Sarah$ $O'Hara$ is a Taylor Swift mega-fan and an assistant editor at Orion Publishing Group.